CW01261082

For Mum

"There's no place like home"

Welcome to

25
UNIQUE
HOMES OF
CHESTER

Lisa Curran,
Currans Unique Homes

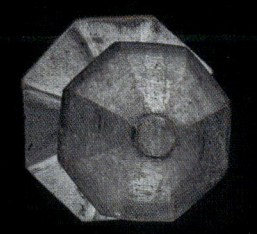

What the owners are saying...

"You have captured my home perfectly. What a wordsmith you are and it feels so true to our discussion, so thank you for listening so well. It's perfect."

"We love the photos so much, your photographer has really made a lot of the house even where we haven't decorated. He's so talented."

"I feel so moved Lisa, I wasn't expecting this. The layout looks beautiful, I'm going to be so proud. Thank you so much for this."

"The photos look stunning. Just makes me realise how lucky we are and have to pinch myself sometimes."

"OMG girl the text is amazing! Wow, you really got me/us. So beautifully and vividly written, you're so talented!"

"Lisa, thank you for making this process so brilliant."

"So emotional – you've done an amazing job – hats off to you all!"

Contents

Preface 5

    Pinfold Farm 6
    Wishing Steps House 14
    Villa Bella Vista 20
    31 Eggbridge Lane 24
    Whitefriars 28
    Cow Lane 34
    Uffington House 40
    Charlton House 46
    Caerlleon 52
    Stretton Hall 56
    Huntington Hall Farm 64
    Gibbet Windmill 70
    Tower House 74
    Kilmorey Lodge 80
    Manor House 84
    Shipgate 90
    The Clock House 94
    Waters Edge 100
    Bridge Place 104
    Dee Bank House 110
    68 Tarvin Road 118
    Woodland House 122
    Sweet Chestnut House 128
    Chester House 134
    35 Dee Banks 140

Acknowledgements 144

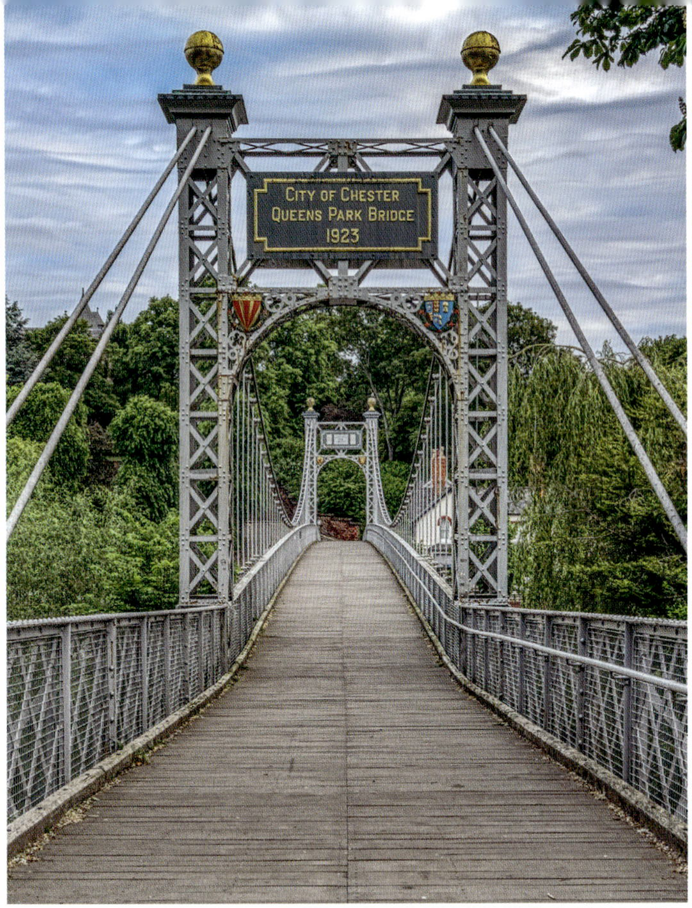
CITY OF CHESTER
QUEENS PARK BRIDGE
1923

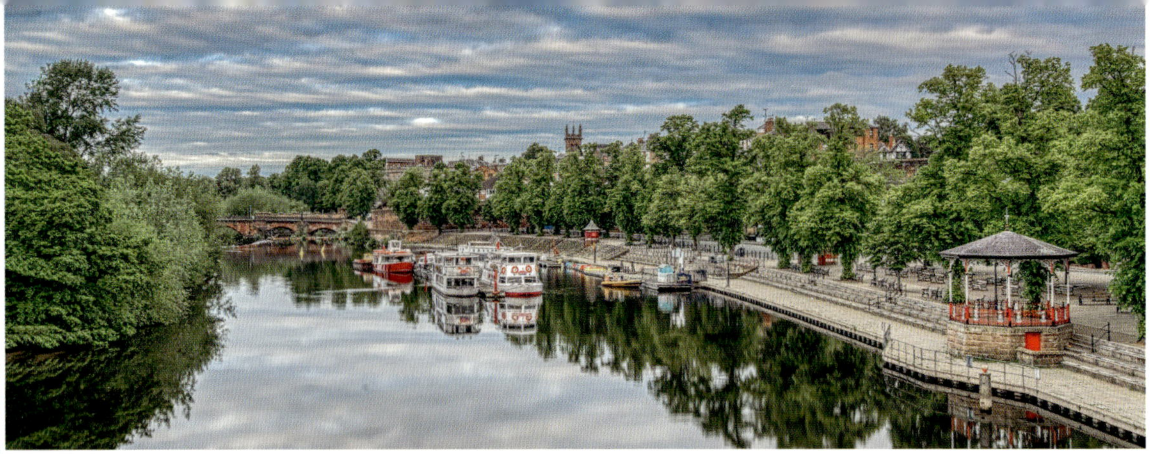

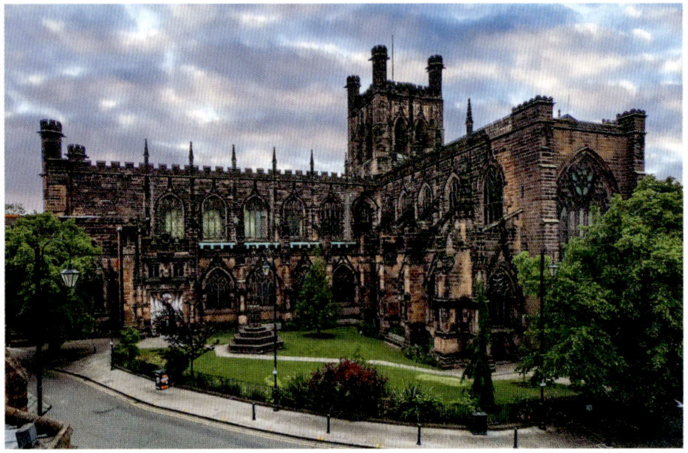

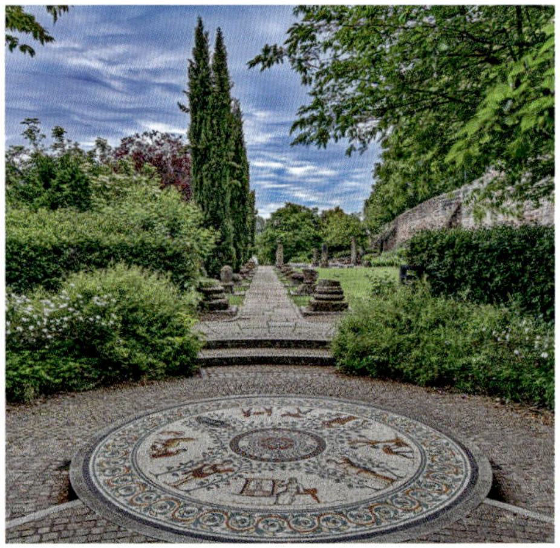

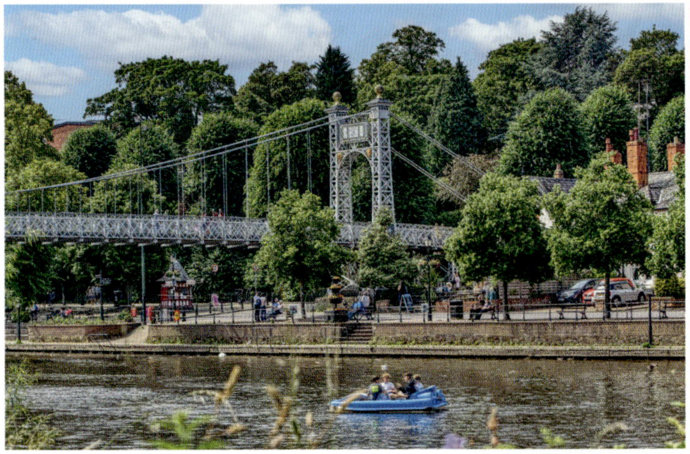

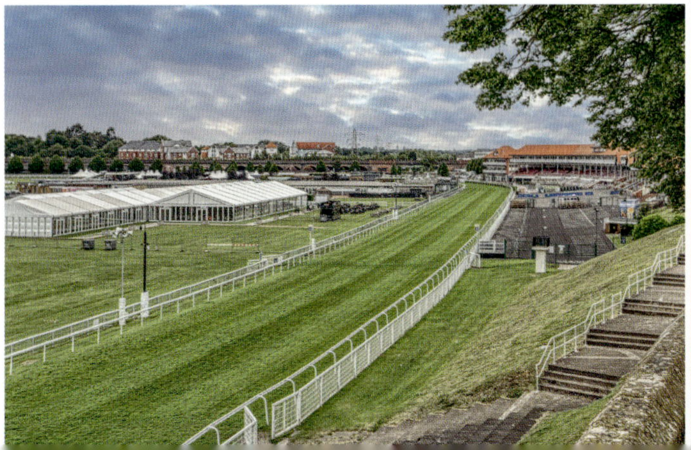

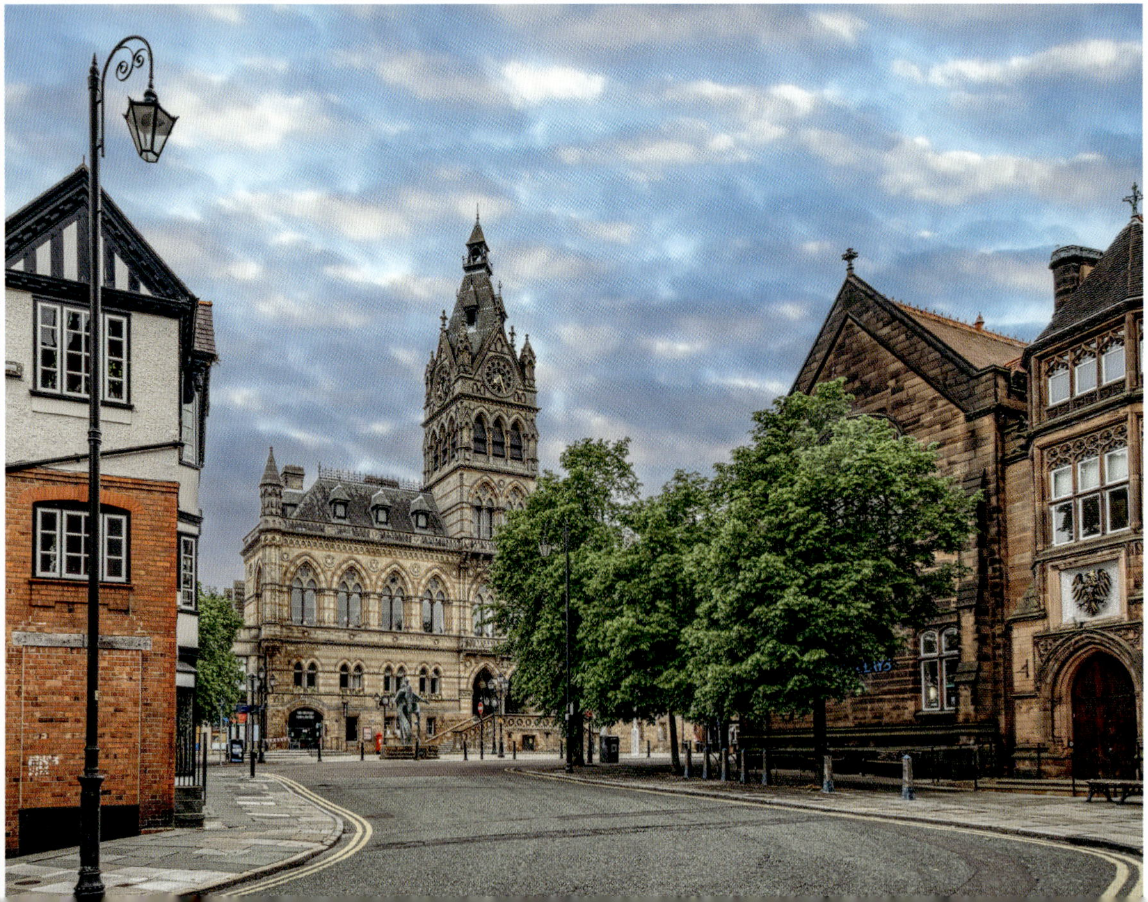

Preface

What does a home want to be?

It's a question that anthropomorphises a building; uncomfortable for some, who believe the anatomy of a home to be limited to gables and bricks, frieze boards and fascias, roof hips and eaves. But then there is the other camp, those who believe in the soul of a home. I must confess, I proudly fall into the latter category.

I am passionate about Chester, and unique homes in equal measure, so compiling this book came as a natural progression, born of the two things that give me such pleasure.

As a working mum, juggling three wonderfully energetic children and a business I love, the quality time spent relaxing at home is crucial. I'm so often told by my clients that their home is their 'haven', 'refuge' or 'sanctuary'. Emotive words, evoking the retreat and safety we find within the walls of the places we call home. The emotional attachment many of us feel toward our homes is profound, perhaps more so now than ever before. As the wider world becomes more unpredictable, we draw our own world more tightly around us, making it a safe space in which we can disconnect from the noise.

Home means different things to different people. And each home in this book is distinctive in its own unique way. Some bigger, some smaller, some rich in history, others new builds, making their debut on the scene. Each home has its own persona, instantly tangible as you step through the door. This palpable sense of personality is as much down to the architectural design and history as it is in relation to the owner, their values, priorities and character as they journey for a time with the house, becoming a part of its process of evolution.

The homes featured in this book are not merely grand homes, or period homes, they are homes that spark joy; unique additions to Chester's landscape, each one with its own story to tell.

We hope you enjoy sharing in their tales as much as we have.

Lisa Curran
Currans Unique Homes

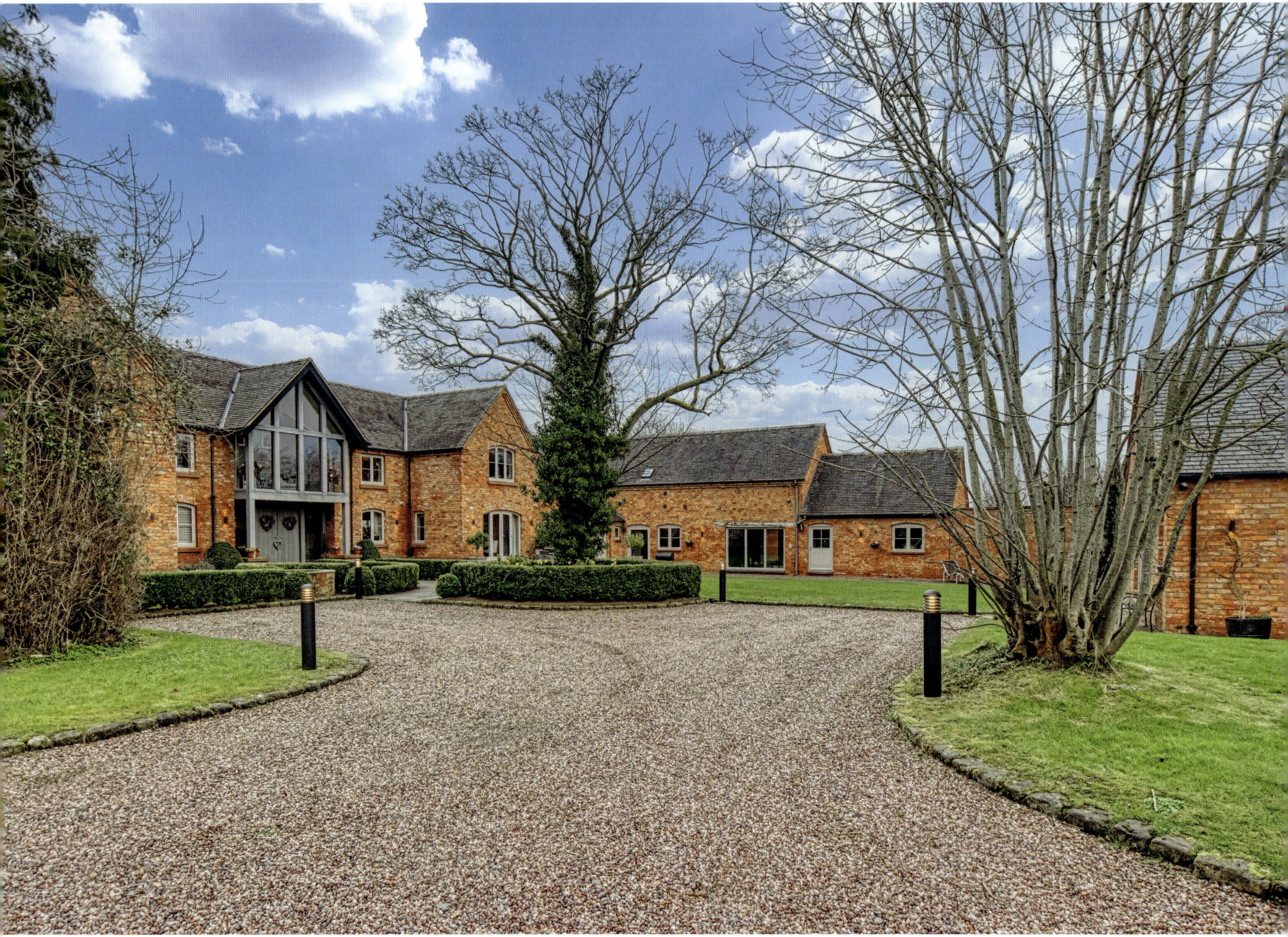

| PINFOLD FARM |

A home in transition...

Originally two farm buildings dating back to the 1800s, Pinfold Farm lies in the picture postcard pretty village of Shocklach, a little over half a mile from the Welsh border. A fresh farmhouse for all intents and purposes, Pinfold Farm in its current incarnation is a little over a decade old, joined together by a central bridging section – sympathetically constructed using characteristic reclaimed red brick for a seamless finish.

Yet, under the custodianship of new owners with an eye for design, room by room, Pinfold Farm is transcending, as a bold new personality is superimposed on its bones. Traditional farmhouse-feel on the outside is juxtaposed by moody boutique chic within, as plush fabrics and dark shades combine with flashes of gold for a luxe ambience.

Original features still convey the depth of its farmhouse character, with thick weathered beams and lintels featured in the entrance hall and piano room.

Fanning out in both directions, one wing lends itself naturally to leisure, accommodating a games room (under the watchful development of a talented interior designer). Spiral stairs lead up to a gym, where full height

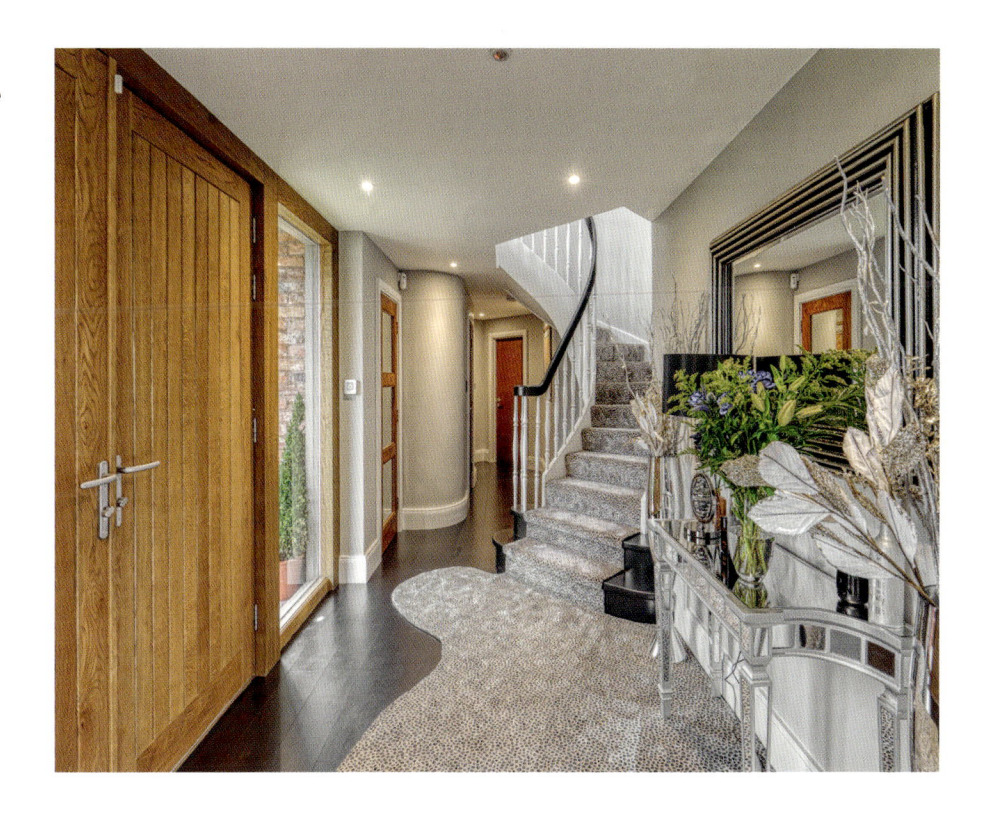

PINFOLD FARM

windows enable workouts taking in the scenery of the Cheshire countryside to a throbbing soundtrack, courtesy of built-in speakers. A home designed to spark joy, a home salon is being introduced, whilst a designated cinema room is spacious, with vaulted ceiling for optimum acoustics, and blackout blinds fitted to the Velux lights.

Pockets of privacy allow adults and children to enjoy moments of quiet; an adult only lounge, dressed in soothing heather tones, lies tucked away beyond the games room providing a haven for grown-ups. Meanwhile, upstairs, the children's bedrooms each contain walk-in wardrobes, ensuite shower rooms and mezzanine level study areas. Grown up privileges in miniature.

Transformed from a dead end into a destination, a bookcase in the corner of the morning room is actually a secret doorway into the study, another moment of metamorphosis for Pinfold Farm.

Practical touches balance the whimsy; an upstairs utility room contains the laundry to one level, whilst plans for a new kitchen reflect a more sociable, real-world style of cooking featuring a bank of waist-height ovens, and a hob on the Italian marble central island facing outward towards guests. Each element in this opulent open-plan space is carefully, precisely sourced, working within the palette of blue-gold-black.

In the master bedroom iridescent gold wallpaper mirroring that at Chanel HQ will dress the feature wall opposite a grand window, framing views over the lake. A menagerie of animal prints sing in symphony, loud

| 25 UNIQUE HOMES OF CHESTER |

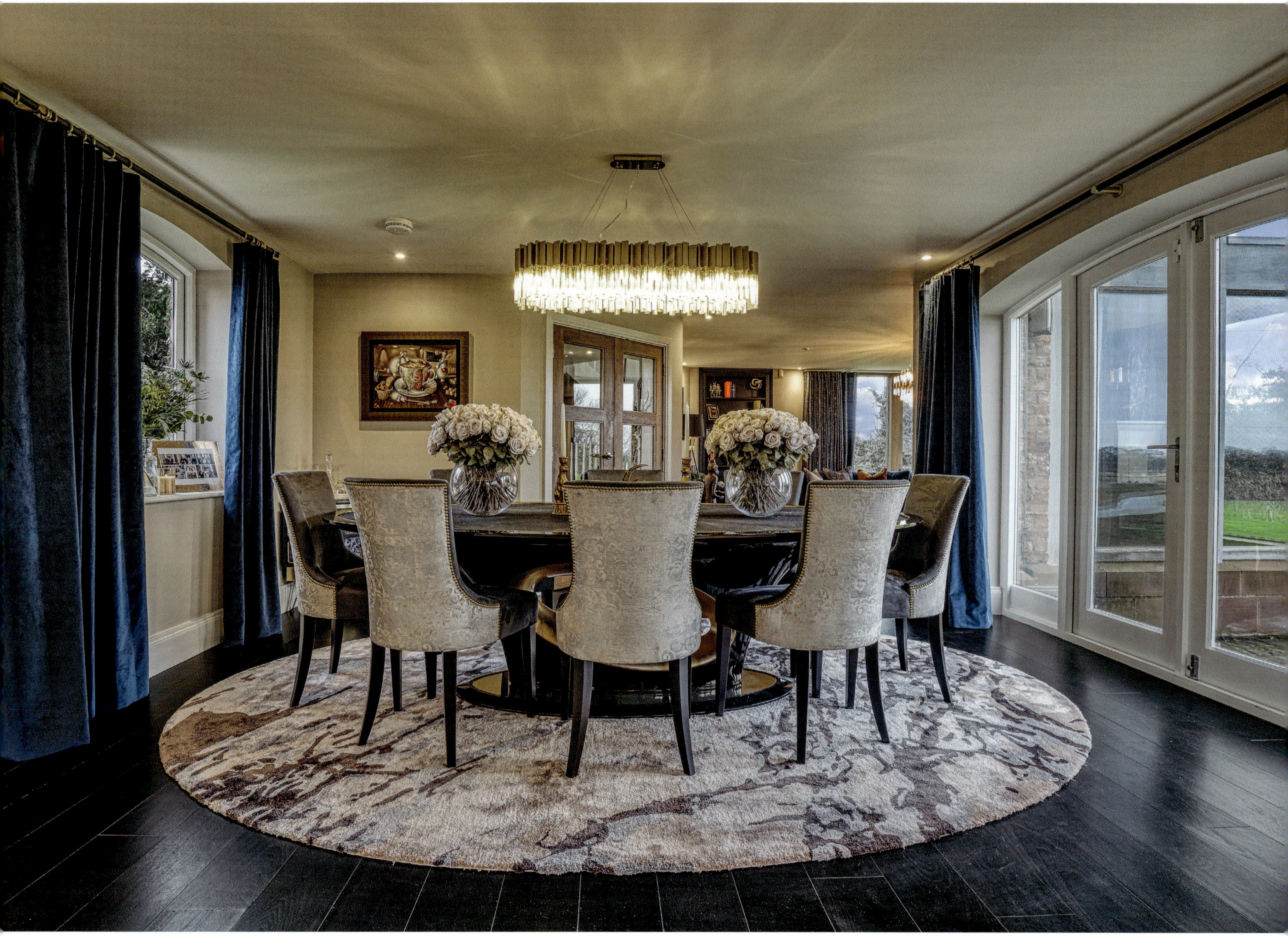

| PINFOLD FARM |

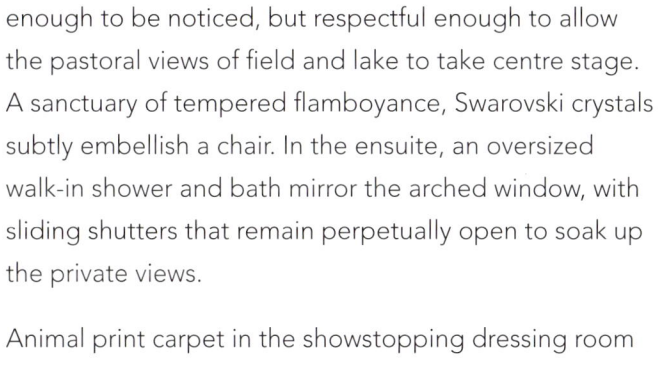

enough to be noticed, but respectful enough to allow the pastoral views of field and lake to take centre stage. A sanctuary of tempered flamboyance, Swarovski crystals subtly embellish a chair. In the ensuite, an oversized walk-in shower and bath mirror the arched window, with sliding shutters that remain perpetually open to soak up the private views.

Animal print carpet in the showstopping dressing room flows out along the landing, cascading down the stairs and puddling at the bottom for maximum impact. Uplighting in doors and windows illuminates Pinfold Farm at night, creating a beacon of comfort to return home to in the distance.

Shining like a sapphire, one area amply lit is the swimming pool; replete with steam room and sauna, it is a highlight of the home, perfect for children's parties and languid summer days. Lighting is key. Following a number of charity events held in the garden, plans are afoot to install permanent uplighting.

Community is at the heart of this home, which, since the arrival of the current owners, is eagerly enveloping the village as a whole into its fold; the inaugural housewarming took the form of a Macmillan coffee morning. Exchanging use of the far field for the maintenance of hedges, employing local, sourcing local, with a focus on give and take within the community, Pinfold Farm is keen to give back to the Shocklach community.

A home with eyes on the future, it is refreshingly defined by what is yet to come - as much in relation to its breadth of footprint, room leading enticingly on to room, as to its

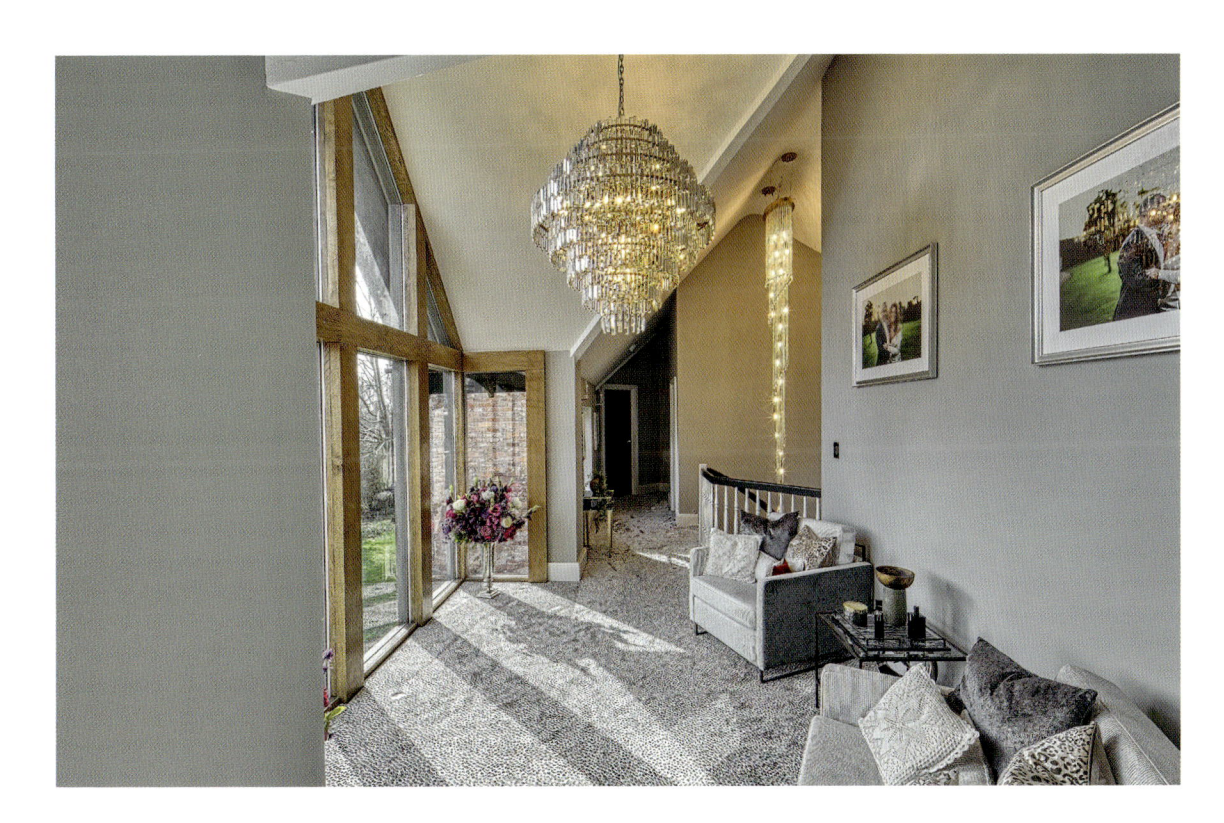

| PINFOLD FARM |

plans, potential and ambition. With space at its behest there are endless layers to be added, from picnic tables and tennis courts to lake view guest accommodation above the garage, and cosy cabanas.

Perhaps one of the most satisfying plans is for the addition of a new gated entrance which will connect the farm to its last remaining field (the former four sold off since the 1930s with each property transaction) via a driveway which will sweep past the lake, uniting the home and land and preserving the privacy and views for generations to come. The field will be forested in order to 'leave something for the future', making good on that commitment to give back.

| 25 UNIQUE HOMES OF CHESTER |

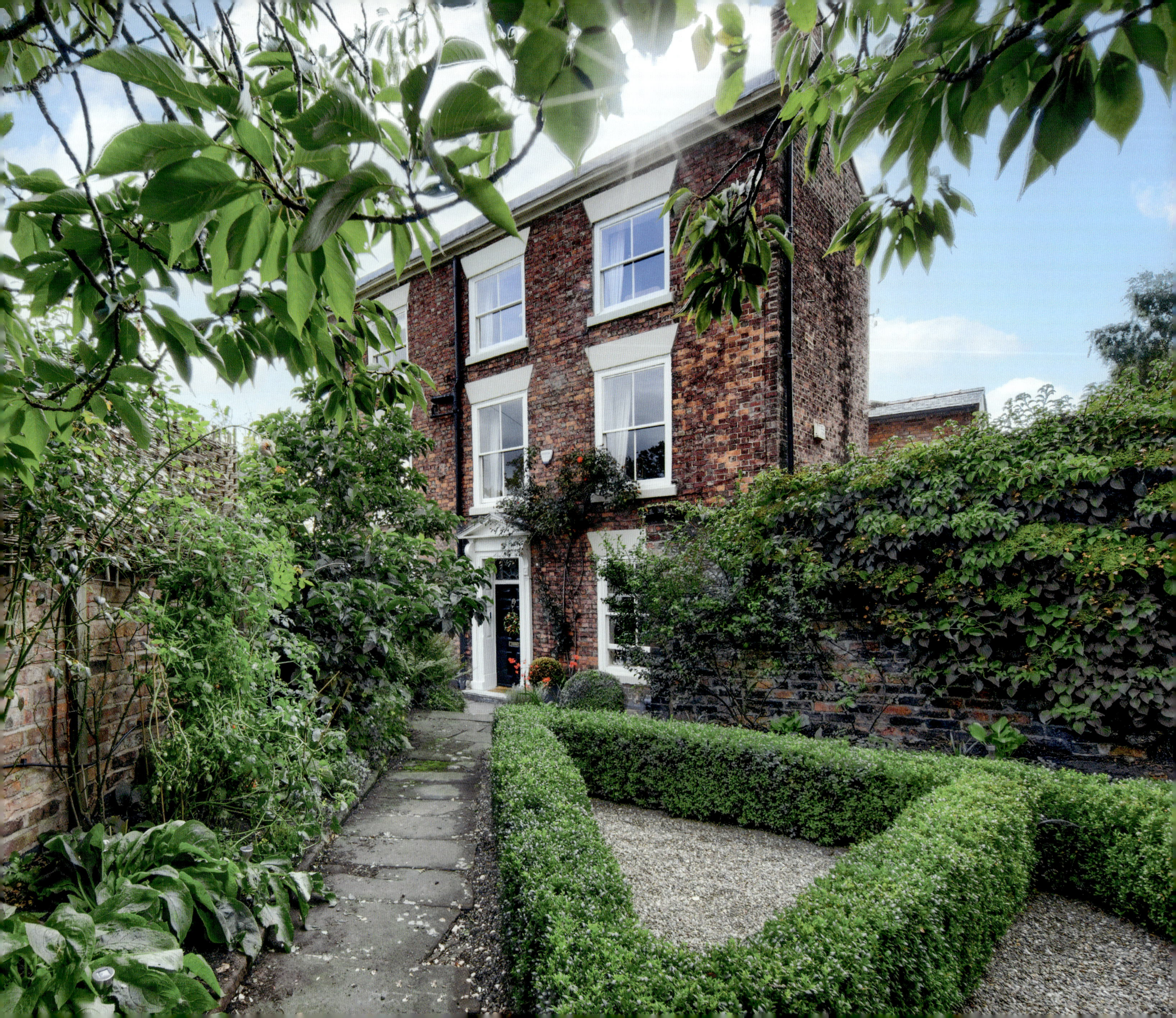

| WISHING STEPS HOUSE |

Hold your breath
and wish upon a stair...

Welcome to the evocatively named and imposingly positioned Wishing Steps House, nestled within the corner of one of Chester's most legendary landmarks.

Steeped in history and mystery, The Wishing Steps, dating back to 1785, run along the south east corner of Chester's ancient walls on route to the Eastgate Clock. Rooted in Chester's mythology and legend, from kissing to wishing, these stone steps are part of the city's fabric.

According to folklore, those who succeed in running up and down the steps whilst holding their breath are granted their wish (rumours hold the original wishers to be wistful women, unmarried and hopeful for husbands).

Utterly unique in its location, Wishing Steps House hugs the corner, its handsomely symmetrical Georgian façade an iconic landmark for those passing by. A fairytale setting, it's impossible not to picture one or two wishes from passersby drifting in the direction of this remarkable home.

WISHING STEPS HOUSE

Poised between the steps and the River Dee, formal gardens replete with box hedging, rambling roses, fragrant wisteria, blossom trees and a private courtyard to the rear capture the essence of quintessential English garden design. Planted to bloom year-round, the garden inspires admiration, setting the perfect scene for the home it celebrates.

An imposing entrance reveals a home true to its history, where original features such as cornicing and fireplaces have been retained in homage to its heritage. Ornately carved, the bannister on the central staircase draws the eye upward: Wishing Steps House is a home yearning to be discovered and explored.

Grand yet homely, recessed bookshelves and Heritage tones from Farrow and Ball create comforting spaces in which to pause and relax. Open coal fires and distinct reception rooms retain the propensity for a traditional way of living, whilst the kitchen with its access to the courtyard garden speaks of a more modern lifestyle.

High ceilings and sash windows evoke the gentleman's residence of yesteryear, with snug lounges and living rooms set over several floors, providing picturesque pockets of privacy from where to look out over the river and walls and savour the city, its past and present.

Waking up to the sound of the river is a daily occurrence, and although its setting by the Wishing Steps is a prominent part of Chester's heritage, the peace and quiet and privacy of Wishing Steps House are all part of its allure. A home with many faces: grand yet homely; private yet a shared landmark of those who know the city, Wishing Steps House is a perfect paradox.

Set beside the reassuring flow of the River Dee and timeless mystique of the Roman walls, Wishing Steps House is a home where setting, landscape, décor and heritage combine to happy effect. Peaceful, prominent and prestigious, it is above all else a much loved and honoured home.

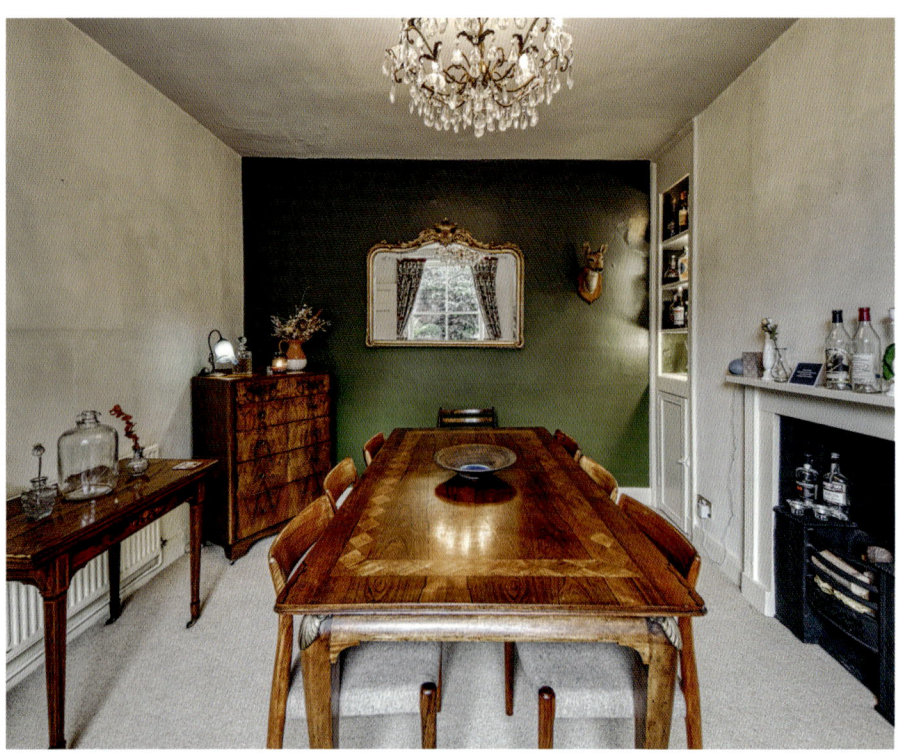

| 25 UNIQUE HOMES OF CHESTER |

| 25 UNIQUE HOMES OF CHESTER |

| WISHING STEPS HOUSE |

| 25 UNIQUE HOMES OF CHESTER |

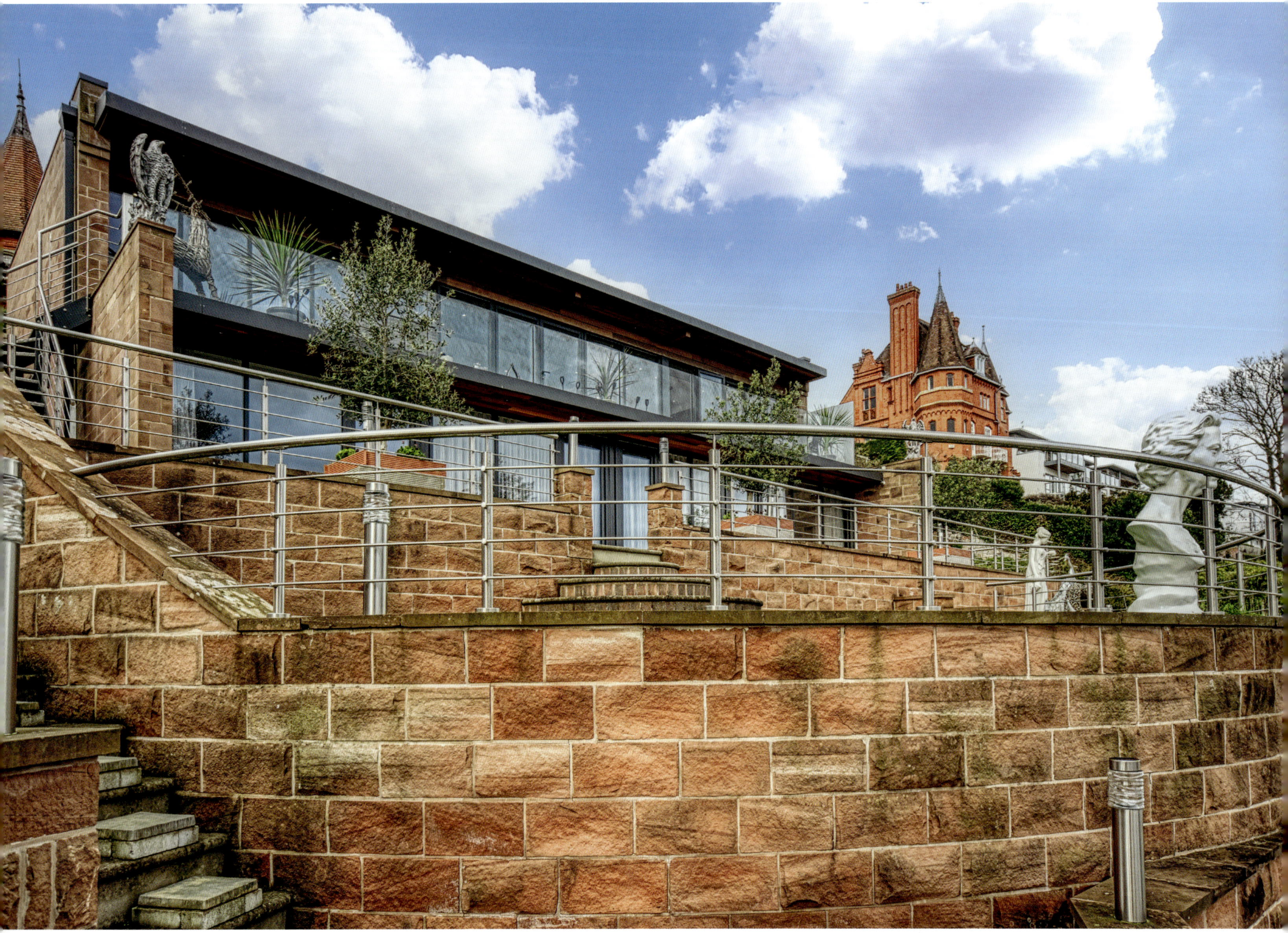

| VILLA BELLA VISTA |

Venetian Vibes
on the banks of the River Dee...

Follow the sunrise from left to right as it melts down over the city, at Villa Bella Vista, a most aptly named home.

Spanish for 'beautiful view', Villa Bella Vista sits on the shores of the River Dee, looking out over the lapping waters to the green expanse of The Meadows beyond.

Influenced and infused with the personality and showmanship of its owner, Villa Bella Vista is set over three levels, with the main living area to the middle, and bedrooms soaking up the munificent views from the upper floor.

A home designed around one concept – entertainment and enjoyment – the lower level, home to an infrared sauna, is soon to see the addition of a resistance swimming pool on the site of what is currently a games room.

The heart of the home is the entrance level, where views over the river and Meadows dominate through floor to ceiling windows spanning the entire width of the home. Open-plan elements are given independence and distinction through subtle changes in décor and flooring. Subdued lighting in the lounge contrasts with the spotlighting, nothing is overlooked in a home where entertaining is more than a hobby, it is a lifestyle.

| VILLA BELLA VISTA |

Bold tones accompany audacious accessories, the influence of one who has spent a lifetime designing rooms and spaces to epitomise daring luxury. Hotel vibes also emanate from the convenient lift connecting the bar, kitchen and living room with the bedrooms above.

Influences from around the globe adorn the gardens at Villa Bella Vista, a treasure trove of mementos from a high-flying life.

Sculptures installed in the garden each tell a tale, illuminated at night for a spectacle of light, shade and shapes. Weatherproof rhinoceroses, Chester's signature animal (black rhinos are a key conservation project for Chester Zoo), once scattered throughout the city have been rehomed in the gardens of Villa Bella Vista, alongside a sculpture of Her Majesty The Queen sourced from The Mill Hotel and Spa.

Casting an utterly unique ambience, tiers of the garden cascade down to the river, another space to entertain and enthral guests. Here, a summerhouse contains its own kitchen and bathroom, allowing for leisurely summer days decamped to the bottom of the garden by the flow of the river. Barbecues in the summertime are mandatory, whilst the pièce de résistance comes, of course, along the river itself.

Making its impressive journey over from the canals of Venice, via Italy, Barcelona, San Sebastian and Plymouth, a little 'piazza' the floating city now bobs about from its moorings at Villa Bella Vista.

Villa Bella Vista, a dream home filled with souvenirs of dreams accomplished, on the banks of the River Dee.

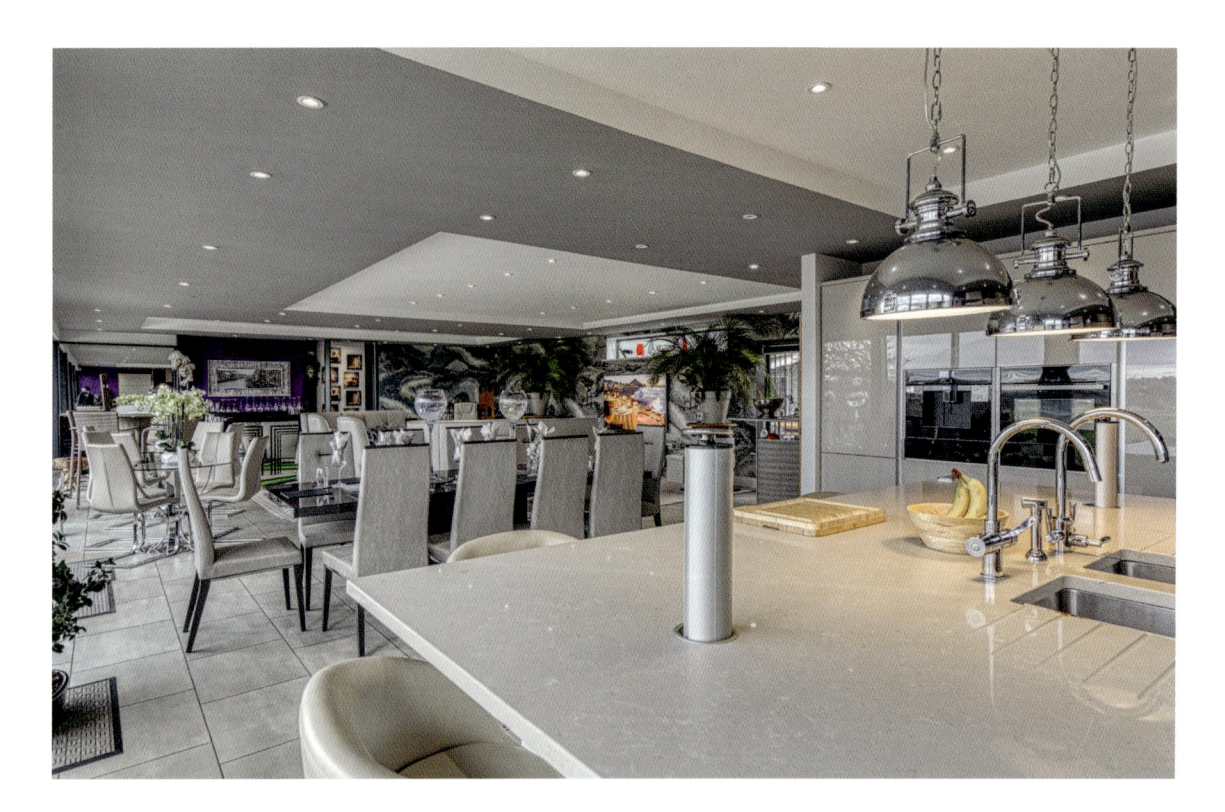

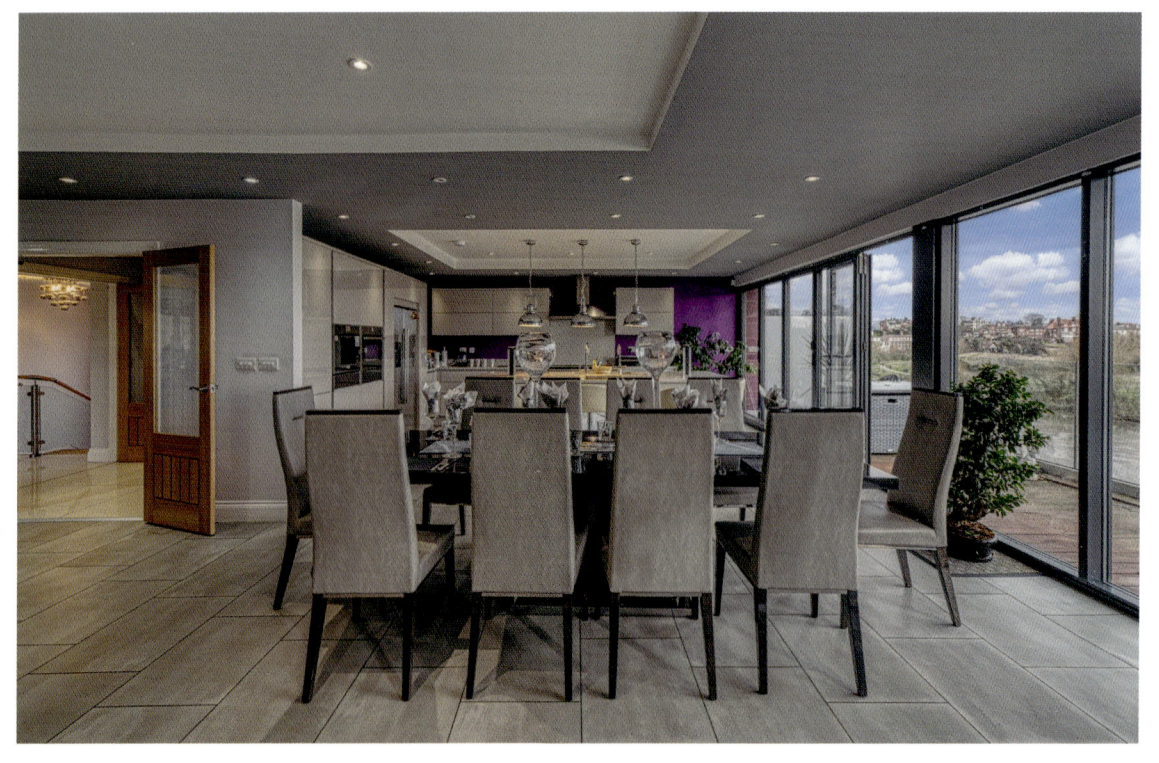

| 25 UNIQUE HOMES OF CHESTER |

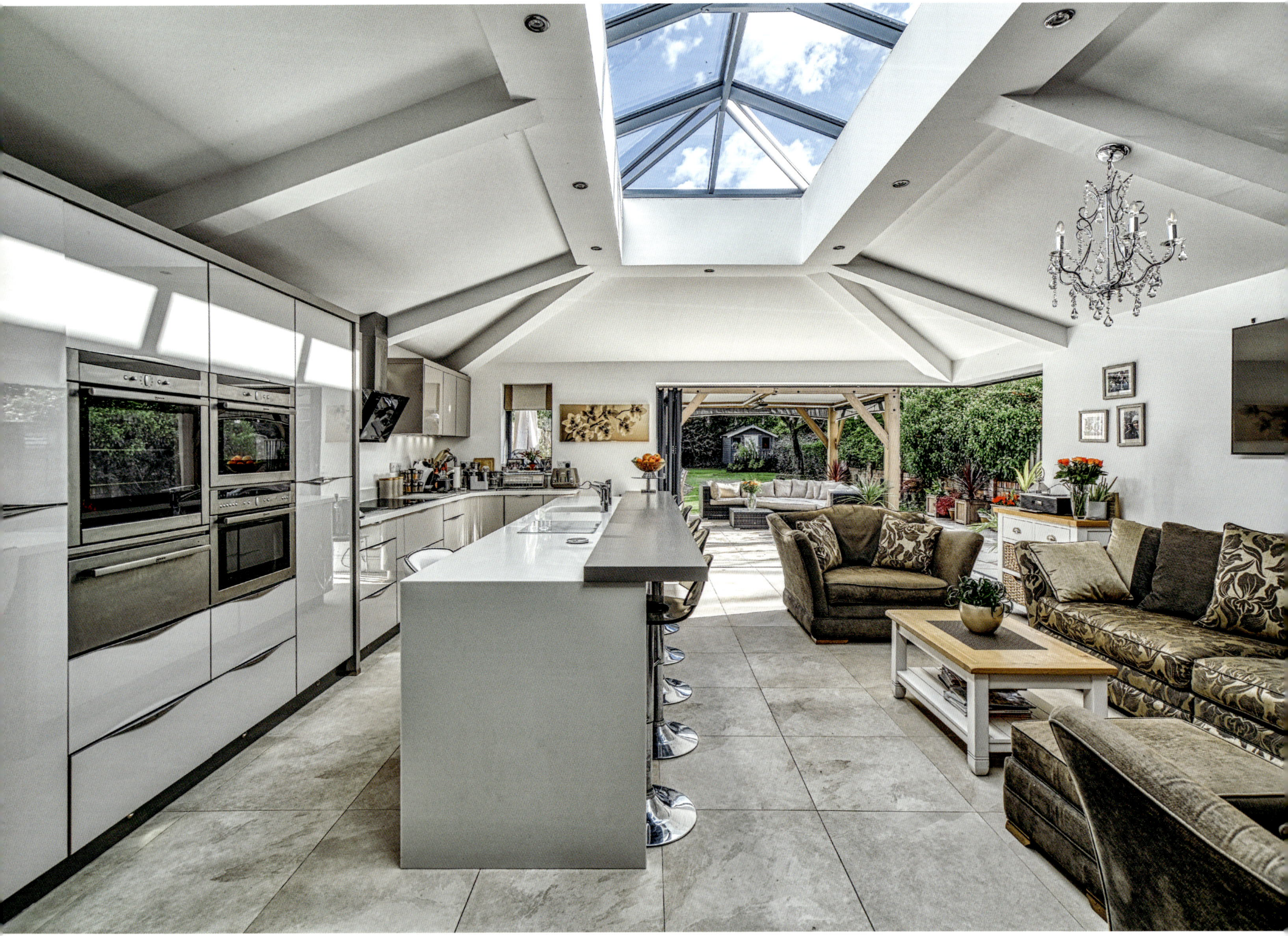

| 31 EGGBRIDGE LANE |

Imperfect,
lived-in perfection to be enjoyed...

Some homes are a destination, ready-made comfort clad in bricks and mortar. Others, a journey, where home and owner grow together creating magical memories on route...

In the Cheshire village of Waverton, No. 31 Eggbridge Lane stands curiously and unpretentiously out from the crowd. Built around 1920, No. 31 only hints at its Edwardian origins from the outside, peacefully set far back from the lane and with its double gable front. With all the playful anticipation of Christmas morning, it keeps its decorative details and period features wrapped up inside.

A home that draws you in, its story is one of evolution, loved initially for its location and potential rather than its modest three-bedroom footprint, No. 31 has grown alongside its owners into a lifestyle home, accommodating the busy needs of a large modern family.

Extensions and changes over time have transformed Eggbridge Lane into a contemporary five-bedroom, three-bathroom, three-storey home, respectfully

31 EGGBRIDGE LANE

reviving a number of original features like the original bannister and stained-glass window in the hallway. What was once a shell in disrepair is now a warm and resonant meeting place; for past and present and for family and friends.

"It's 'lived in'– that's what a home is about. What's the point in its creation if people can't relax?"
- Homeowner

Perhaps the mood of this home is attributable to the changes made and the convivial lifestyle the adjustments afford: walls altered and moved to create connected spaces such as the living and dining rooms, linked by a feature glass tunnel fire, imported from Belgium. Standing in place of the traditional fire and chimney, convenient and captivating, the contemporary fire diffuses heat to both rooms simultaneously and creates a stunning focal point from both sides.

Bespoke wall murals and bold colours create rooms with atmosphere and personality. Upstairs, further extensions see a master bedroom with its own balcony, ensuite and dressing room where full length mirrors create a real feeling of space and light in true funhouse fashion.

But it is the spaces designed to draw people together which truly distinguish this home, the highlight of which is undoubtedly its rear extension and kitchen. Complete with glass atrium and bifold doors opening onto the outside area, this family hub also has an island ranging over 3.5 metres in length with adjoining breakfast bar. The heart of the home, designed to accommodate and entertain, a robust solid wood gazebo and outdoor kitchen have been created beyond the bifolds, bespoke built for milestone birthday celebrations and maximum sociability. No. 31 is a home where the on-holiday vibe is an emanation of its design.

A lifestyle home, independent spaces accompany social meeting points, with older teenagers afforded the entire top floor bedrooms and bathroom to themselves. Peaceful pockets filled with light allow for quiet contemplation and work throughout the day, before the home fills with clamour and laughter after 3pm.

Glamour entwines with family reality at No. 31, a handsome and homely haven whose garden sign 'our space is a place where friends and family gather, and love grows' is the perfect epitaph for this home on Eggbridge Lane: imperfect, lived-in perfection to be enjoyed.

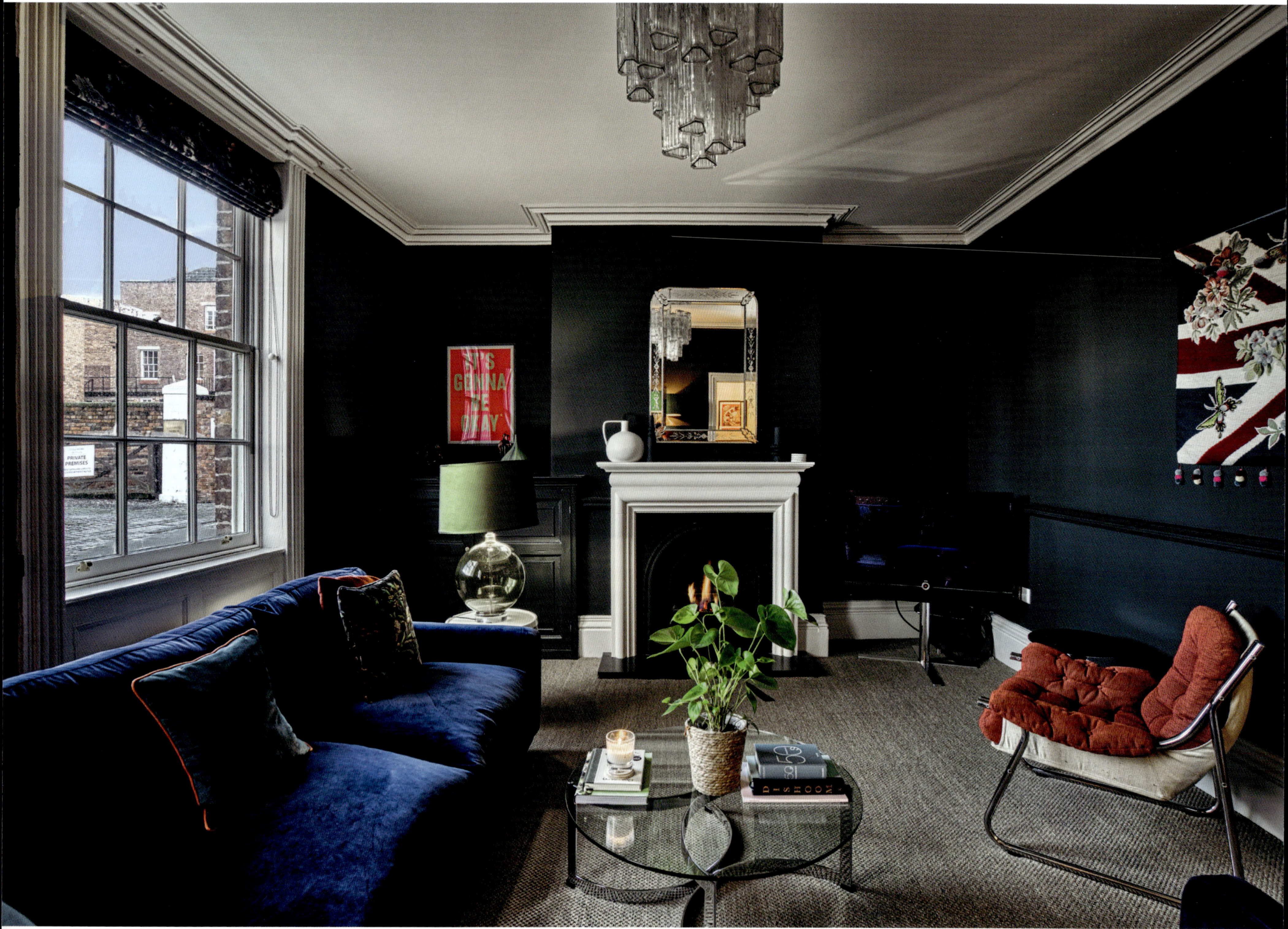
IT'S GONNA BE OKAY
PRIVATE PREMISES
DISHOOM

| WHITEFRIARS |

A party home
with great bones...

The epitome of Georgian townhouses, all rise for Whitefriars, a former solicitors' office reimagined as a warm family home in the heart of the city.

Combining centrality with tranquility, find Whitefriars nestled at the quieter end of a quaint cobbled street, only sixty seconds from the hustle and bustle of Chester, where wine bars, theatres, cinemas and boutiques abound.

There is a sense of solemnity looking up at Whitefriars, its handsome collection of symmetrical sash windows gazing down alongside its grand and imposing Regency entrance; a traditional six-panel front door embellished by columns, pediments and crown mouldings, austere as a robed judge beneath his ceremonial wig.

Through the threshold, Whitefriars remains true to its bones, down in no small part to its current owners. Painstakingly and patiently restored to its former glory, original Minton flooring has been meticulously removed, restored and re-laid in its previous pattern. Above and below, where the Georgian skirting boards and mouldings had been damaged or removed, handmade plaster replicas have been commissioned. Each single glazed window to the front has been carefully restored.

| WHITEFRIARS |

Not only a commercial property but also a listed building, plans to transform Whitefriars into a family home all pivoted on one crucial hinge; the removal of a key wall to create a contemporary kitchen-diner for modern open-plan living.

The result? A decadent yet informal living, cooking and dining space. Classic Shaker style units are given a contemporary twist, finished in Farrow & Ball's dramatic 'Railings', whilst the marbled worktops are a bold work of art, a fine tribute to the grandeur and size of the home.

A family home at heart, retreat to the snug where velvet textures and inky tones dominate, warmed by the roaring open fire…an intimate and cosy room.

Sociable by design, nights in become nights out, where a second floor devoted to entertainment accommodates its own bar and lounge. The dress and design of the large lounge celebrates the eclectic styles of its owners, perhaps echoed in the original detailed coving which remains. With typical city views characteristic of Whitefriars' roots, large sash windows frame views out over a handsome and historic solicitors' office alongside its verdant lawn and ancient trees.

Whitefriars is also a family home, soaking up residents by providing pockets of privacy and refuge; each of the five bedrooms, discovered on split levels, is served by its own luxurious ensuite.

Yet, it is outdoors where Whitefriars' most unique and creative qualities can be best appreciated.

A vision of architecture, a small area 15 feet beneath the level of the home has been transformed into a triple

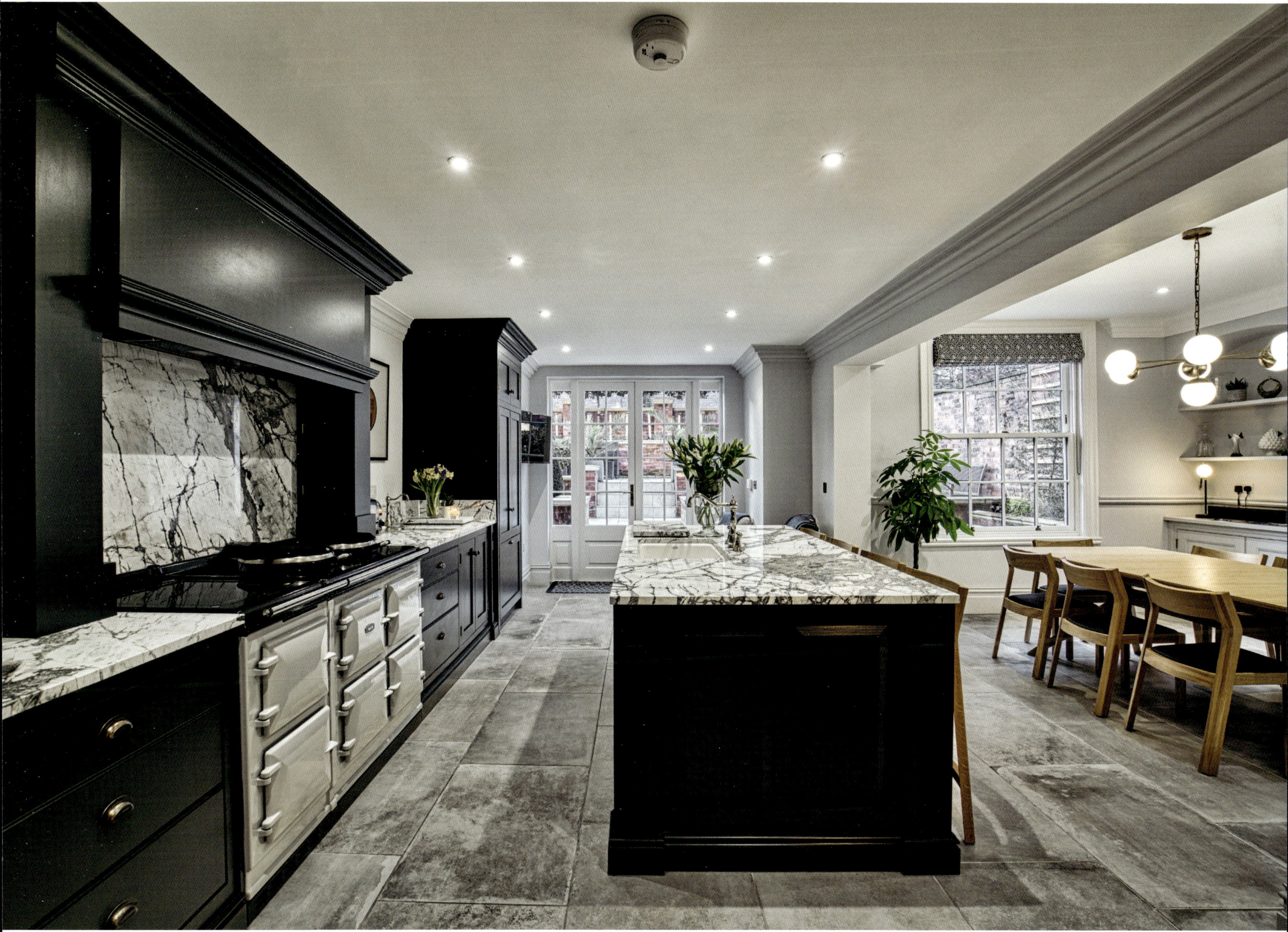

| 25 UNIQUE HOMES OF CHESTER |

WHITEFRIARS

garage – a rarity in the city centre. Optimising the space, a steel framework was constructed to accommodate a tiered garden above; essentially creating a floating walled garden sanctuary – reclaiming space from thin air. Designed to delight with year-round greenery providing privacy and screening, classic tones of lavender and white fill the air with summer fragrance. Bifold doors recede to create the indoor-outdoor living demanded in this brave new world where one's home truly is one's castle.

Whitefriars is the epitome of a success story. A rescue mission accomplished by risktakers with real vision, now rewarded with an utterly unique city centre home which celebrates and safeguards its heritage for future generations.

Homely, comforting and family-oriented, Whitefriars is both a sanctuary and a party home, with the excitement of Chester only a few steps away.

25 UNIQUE HOMES OF CHESTER

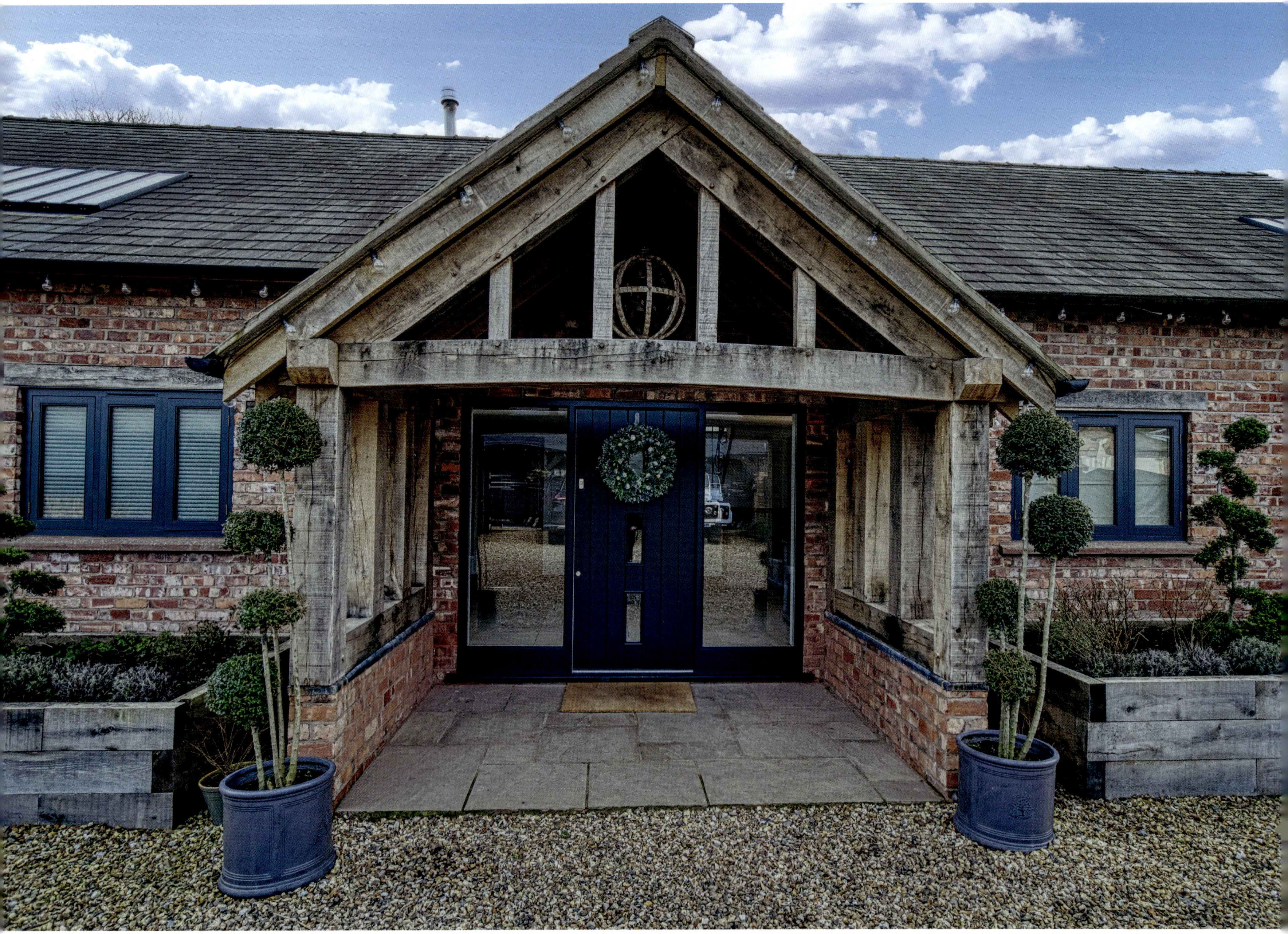

| COW LANE |

A Cinderella story...

Some homes, like people, are born into luxury; destined for merchants, aristocrats and even royalty. For others, it's a process of evolution, a Cinderella story.

In fairy-tale fashion, along Cow Lane, stands a vision of glass, oak and rustic red brick - sprung from humble origins.

Born a cow shed in the late 1800s, this byre was converted to residential use in the early 2000s before being renovated once more in 2017. While traits of its modest beginnings remain in the original brick pillars along the rear and the sturdy oak beams in the kitchen, so respectful has been the re-modelling work, and so well matched the materials, it is impossible to distinguish old from new in this inspired transformation.

On approach, the height of the newly installed trio of dormer windows and large outdoor entertaining hut provide a tantalising taste of what is to come. The gabled oak portico is an architectural statement, adding definition to the front of the home.

| COW LANE |

Inside, the wow factor is arguably not the polished oak and curved steel of the bespoke staircase and galleried landing, illuminated by unique, imported Italian lighting, but the homely warmth that pervades. Testament in part to the subtlety of design and styling (and underfloor heating), and respect for the truth of the home; the gentle bow of the railings is evocative of the mangers which would once have stood here. Earthy tones and red brick fireplaces embracing log burners paint an easy palette of 'contemporary-country' throughout.

Where other renovations remove walls to create open-plan spaces, partitions have been introduced to create pockets of privacy whilst remaining airy and light due to the scope and size of the rooms, resulting in a practical home, with fantastic flow for entertaining.

Bountiful bedrooms soak up the extensive countryside views, elevated by newly installed dormers, an aesthetic move to create balance in the visual effect from

| 25 UNIQUE HOMES OF CHESTER |

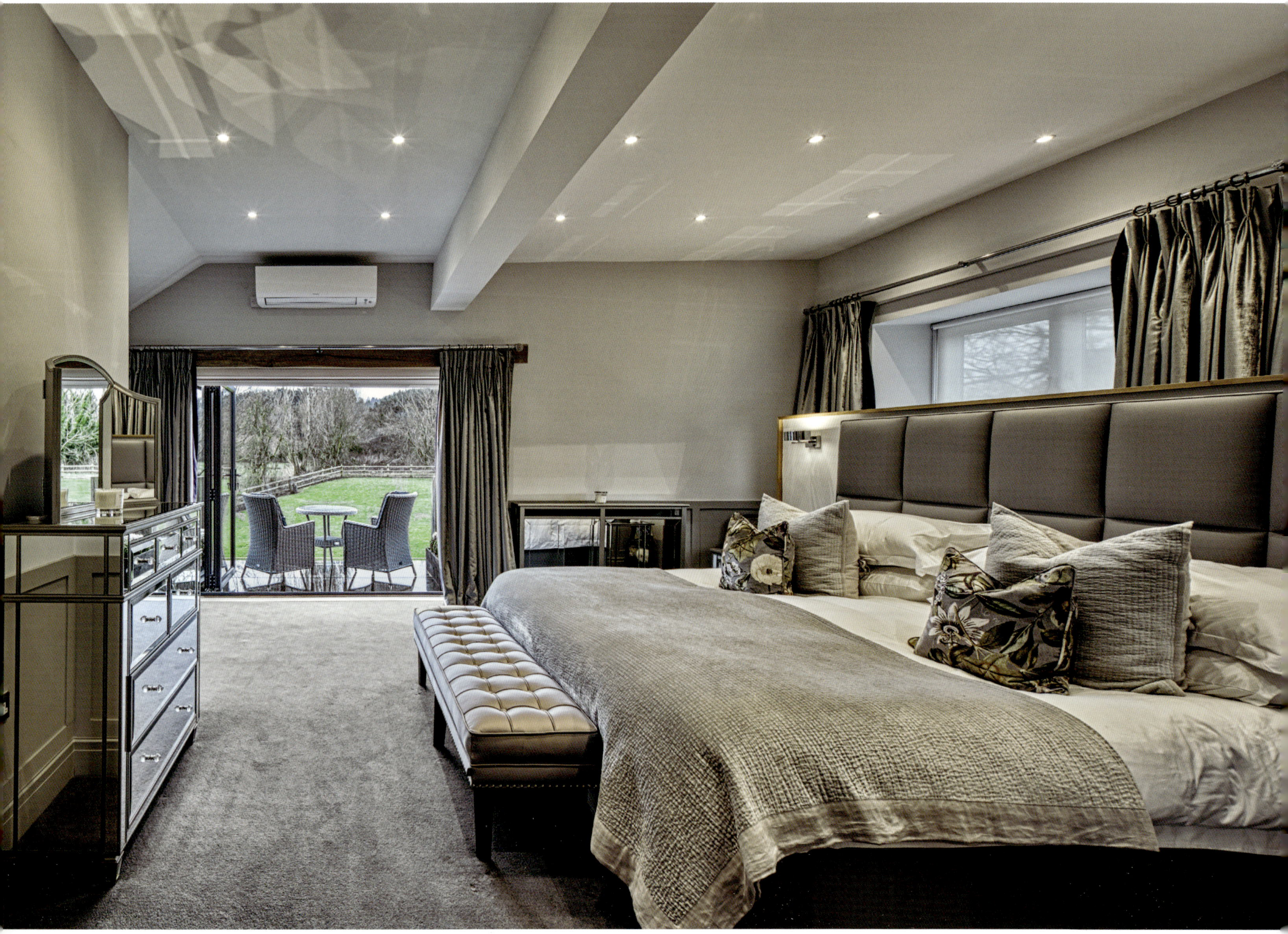

| COW LANE |

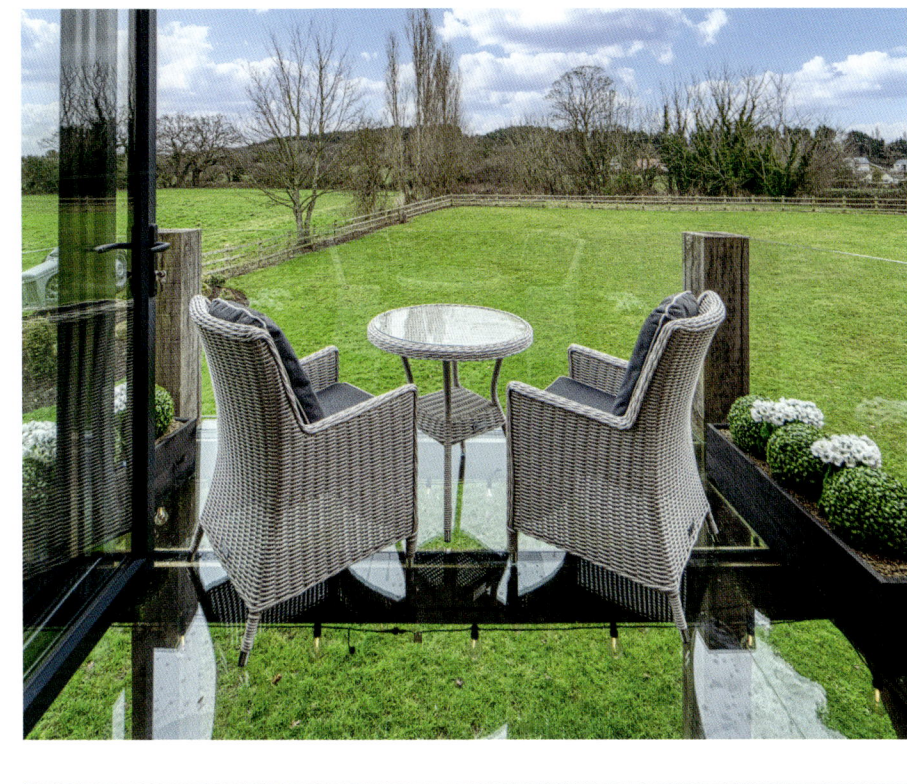

the rear. Soothing sanctuaries all, the master in particular is a joy to behold, with its glass floor balcony offering a seamless connection to the countryside and allowing light to flow unencumbered into the lounge below.

Served by a bar indoors and out, entertaining is at the heart of this home. Fully landscaped, the grounds have been designed in stages from driveway to decking, incorporating an illuminated feature rockery inspired by the Hampton Court Flower Show; there is an element of fun to this masterpiece home. This is a place for outdoor dinner parties and festive fetes, a warm and inviting home, at its best when filled with the resonance of laughter and revelry.

Property, like people, performs at its best when it is shown kindness and respect, a truth demonstrated happily at Cow Lane; a barn that remains a barn, whilst having at once become so much more.

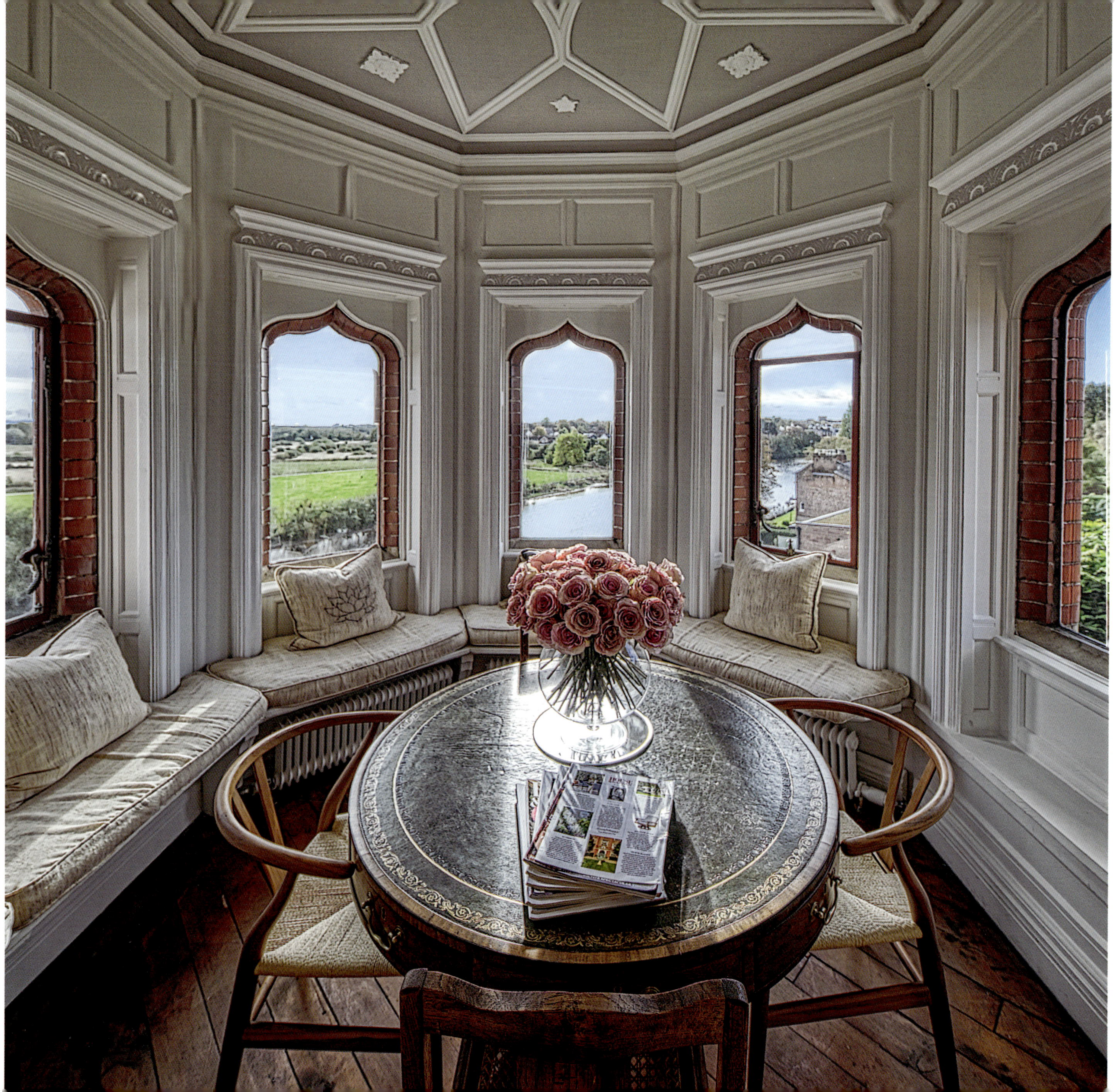

| UFFINGTON HOUSE |

Chester's not-so-secret castle...

A remarkable feat of architecture along the River Dee, so captivating is Uffington House with its handsome stone mullion windows, castellated turrets, and lead finial accented spires, it is affectionately referred to by locals as 'the castle'. Nestled between two turrets, and flanked protectively by a pair of carved stone lions, there is more than an air of regality to this majestic Chester home.

Designed by Edward Ould, pupil of renowned Chester architect John Douglas, Uffington House was built in 1885 for Thomas Hughes, author of Tom Brown's Schooldays, and named after the village in which he was born.

Its Grade-II listing is evident in the architectural triumphs presenting themselves even before setting foot across the threshold. With or without its listing, there is a clear sense of duty and responsibility felt by its owners to respect, maintain and preserve this unique home for generations to come.

Identifying the 'star quality' of Uffington House is an impossible task, instead the elements work in harmony to create a home impossible to recreate. Turrets that diminish in size as the home rises up; the magnificent central solid oak staircase, intricately carved, ascending through all three floors; ornate

UFFINGTON HOUSE

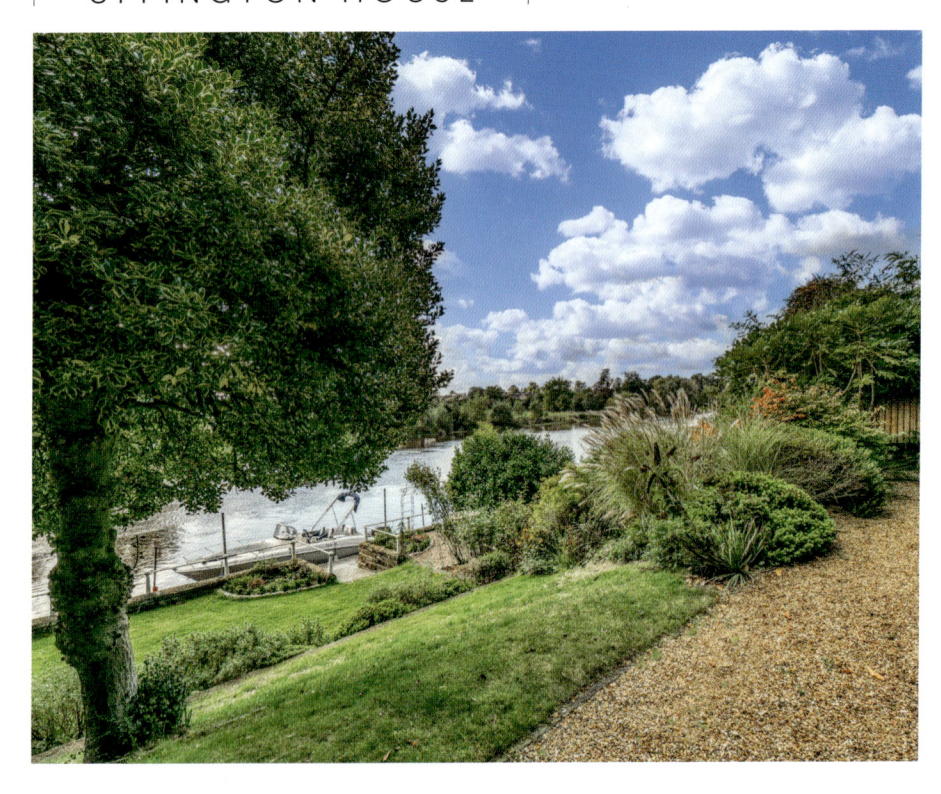

plaster ceilings; the contemporary entertaining kitchen where oversized stone mullion windows frame views over the River Dee and the peaceful Meadows. Beauty abounds at every turn.

Given its wealth of features, perhaps it is surprising to note the internal shifts at Uffington House. In recent years the kitchen, the modern-day hub of the home, has been cleverly relocated to maximise the river views. On the penthouse level, a master bedroom, a dressing room and ensuite occupies the whole of the third floor, whilst the slipper bath in the ensuite drinks in views over the river and Meadows. A one-bedroom apartment with its own separate entrance has been created to allow guests total privacy.

Yet for all its its grandeur and size, Uffington House remains to all intents and purposes a practical and embracing home. Eclectically dressed, flow from formality to fun, classic to contemporary throughout the rooms at Uffington House, whose large walls offer a blank canvas upon which the custodians can imprint their own personality. Like a fashion model, whatever Uffington House is dressed in, it simply serves to enhance its natural beauty.

| 25 UNIQUE HOMES OF CHESTER |

43

A glass of wine is best enjoyed from the upstairs drawing room, where two large sets of doors lead out to a double wrought iron balcony, offering remarkable vistas over the river, set 250ft above its steady flow.

Outside the garden offers a tiered approach to the river, where moorings allow for swift access to the river and Meadows. Embracing river life is part and parcel of Uffington House, from witnessing the rowers strike out across the water, to observing ducks bobbing by, and even catching the occasional triathalon. A focal point for tourists on the pleasure boat tours, pockets of privacy in the garden provide peace in this outdoor oasis.

Unequivocally unique, Uffington House is more than a quirky feat of architecture, it is, by admission of those privileged to care for it, the most beautiful, tranquil and peaceful home imaginable. Inimitable, original and historic, Uffington House is a bastion of serenity in the city.

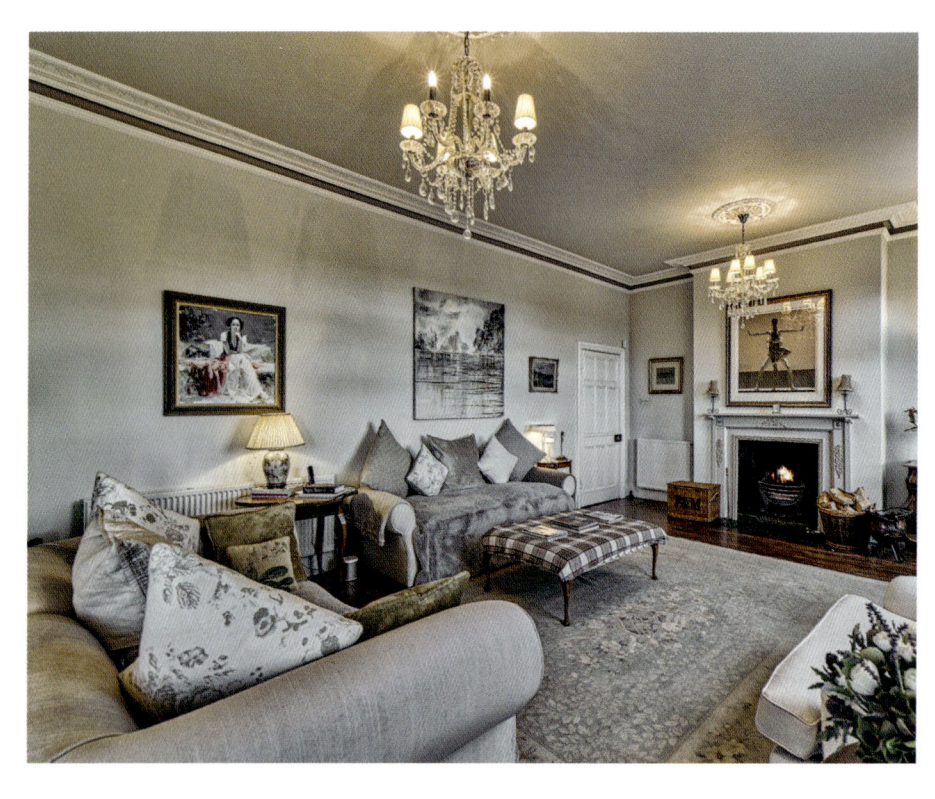

| UFFINGTON HOUSE |

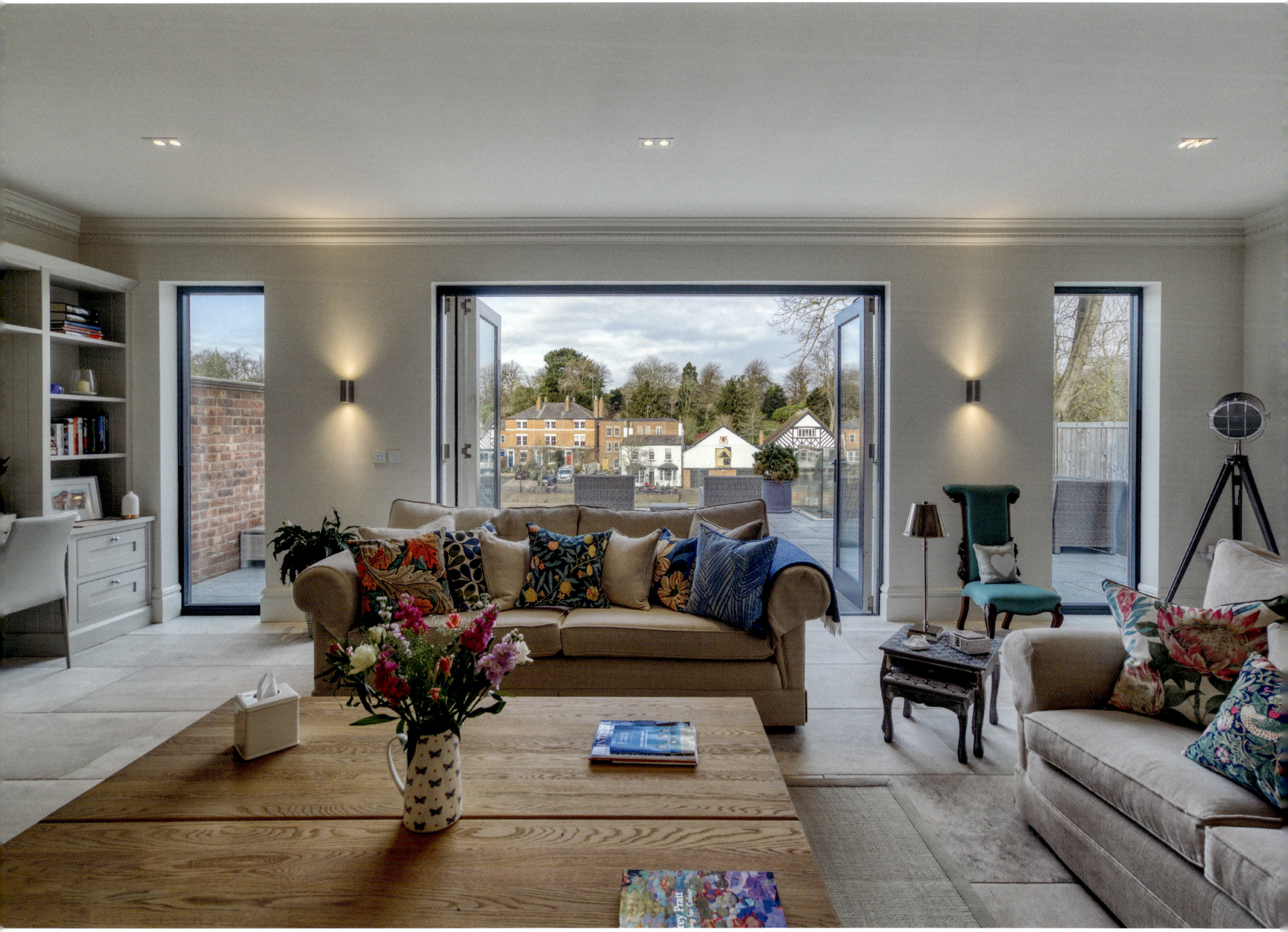

| CHARLTON HOUSE |

A modern addition to Chester's riverscape...

With its rich Roman heritage, period properties rightfully adorn Chester's cobbled streets like a finely woven tapestry, time capsules in tribute to the city's past. But across the river from this eclectic collection, stands a new build townhouse keen to make its own mark in the annals of history.

Those unfamiliar with the locale are surprised to find that Charlton House looks out over the river. Tucked behind a pristinely paved and gated driveway off Lower Park Road, its austere Georgian-style front door, lending it a healthy dose of gravitas, opens to reveal a formal dining hall in the first instance.

Cloud-like combinations of greys and whites converge with chic lighting from Chester's designer furniture specialist Chattels to set a soothing scene. A motif continued throughout Charlton House, the marbled tones of the porcelain tiles meet with plush silver carpet in the snug lounge and bedrooms. Formality flows upward in the stylish stair runner, secured with brushed chrome rods.

| CHARLTON HOUSE |

The pristine palette provides the perfect blank canvas, allowing the personality of the home and its residents to shine through in a colourful injection of art, fresh flowers and vibrant soft furnishings.

Underfloor heating also counters the cool white, infusing warmth throughout the first two levels. Beyond broad double doors ahead, an impressive stone fireplace also adds old-school ambience, its log burner a festive feature giving a focal point to this grand space.

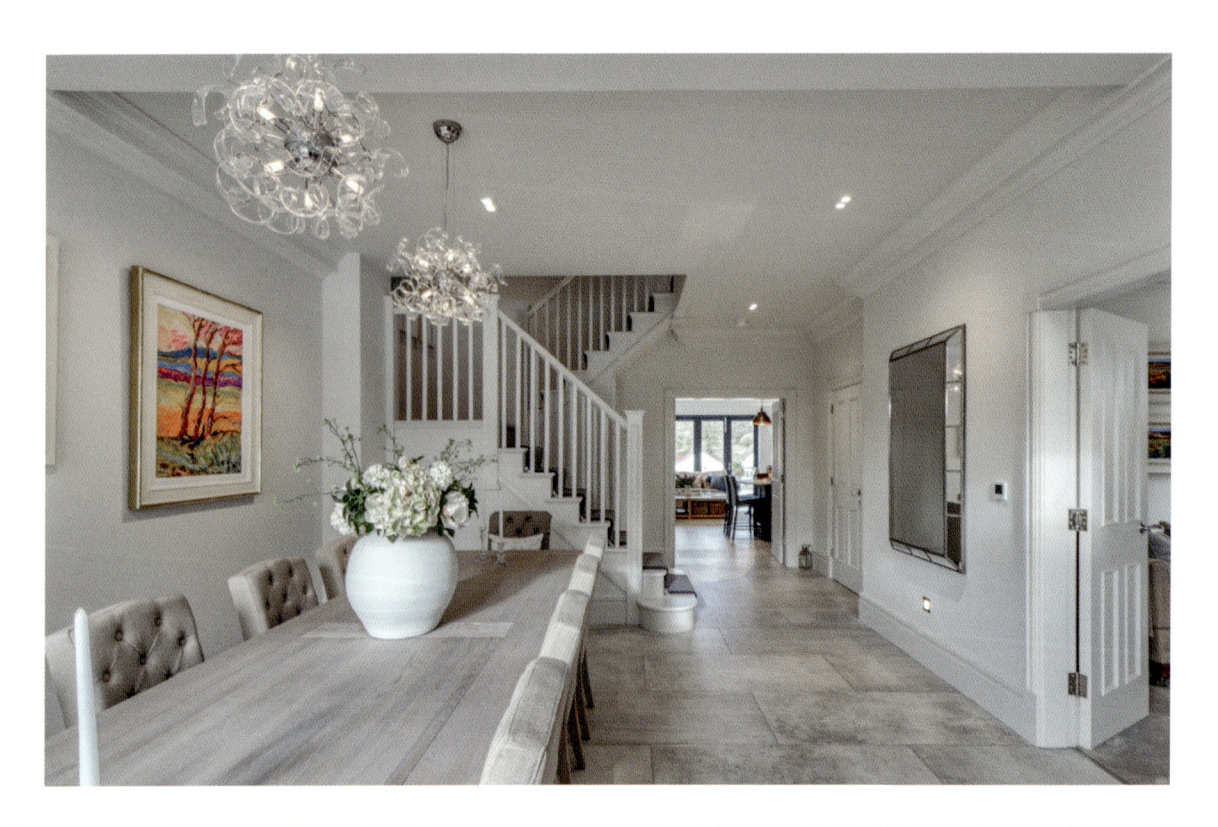

The heart of the home, the open-plan living-kitchen-dining room is the essence of contemporary living: sociable, spacious and scenic, a wall of glass draws the riverside indoors, seamlessly linking to the glass fronted terrace outside. Here, beyond the bifolds, in the height of summer, sunshine warms the stone of the terrace until evening; a balmy viewing platform to watch the world float by until sun sets over the river. Steps lead down to a lower garden, beyond which there is access to the river.

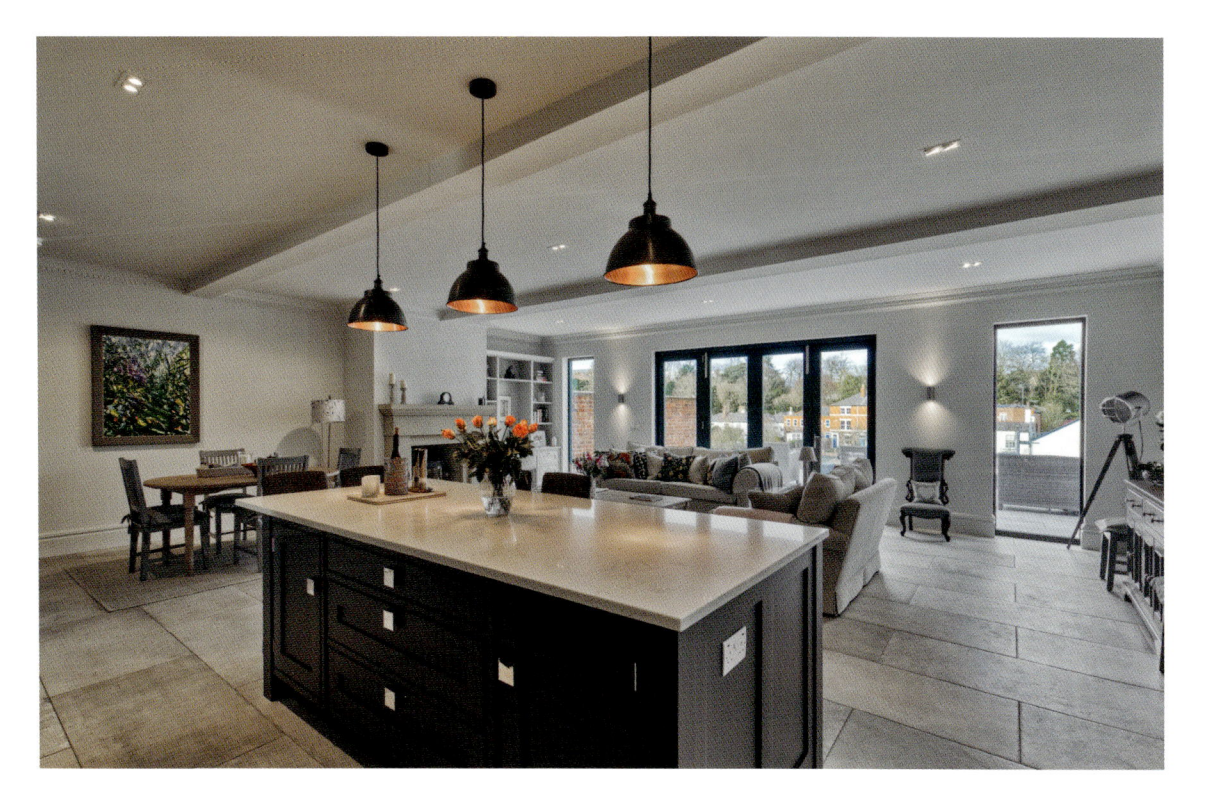

To one corner, a bespoke study area connects with the Shaker style cabinetry of the kitchen, continuing the comforting consistency which defines Charlton House. Key furniture and accessories sourced from Neptune and Oka add a brushed, beach vibe for a homely feel. Cushions, rugs and cleverly placed lamps; like a gourmet salad, serve as the dressing that brings out the flavour of this home.

Slip away to the snug, where cosy carpet and Duresta fabrics accompany an oversized duck egg and cream futon commissioned to fit the room perfectly. No decorative detail is overlooked at Charlton House, each item, carefully considered, takes its role in the overall scheme, combining to create a subtle masterpiece of homely comfort.

On the first floor, the master bedroom is a vision of soothing luxury; low key furnishings standing in the background, deferring to the prominent river views, best enjoyed from the balcony. At night, picture postcard views of the bridge, illuminated, are a reminder of the utterly unique and privileged outlook of this home. Only a walk away, Chester's magic glow beckons…the gateway to the city only a few steps from the front door.

With five bedrooms over two storeys, Charlton House somehow retains its intimate feel. Doors perpetually open, each casing framing snapshot views of a familyoriented, sociable home.

Spotless, genial and on the expressive side of minimal, Charlton House effortlessly weaves itself into the weft of Chester's unique riverscape.

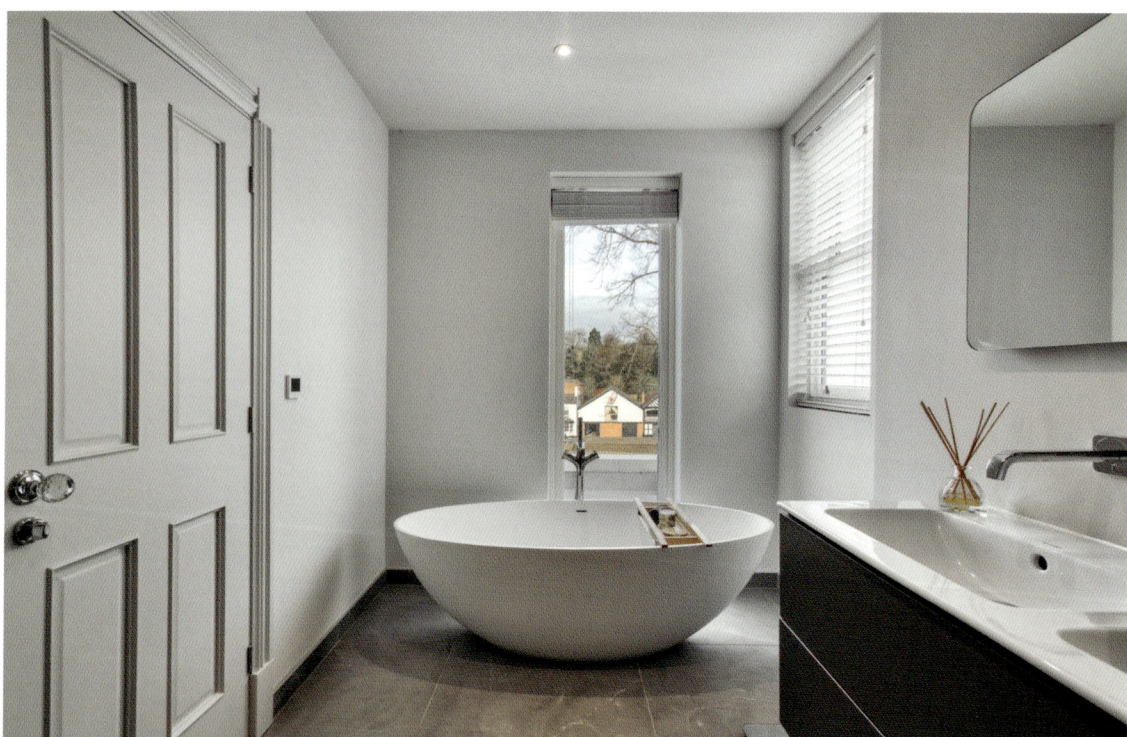

| 25 UNIQUE HOMES OF CHESTER |

| CHARLTON HOUSE |

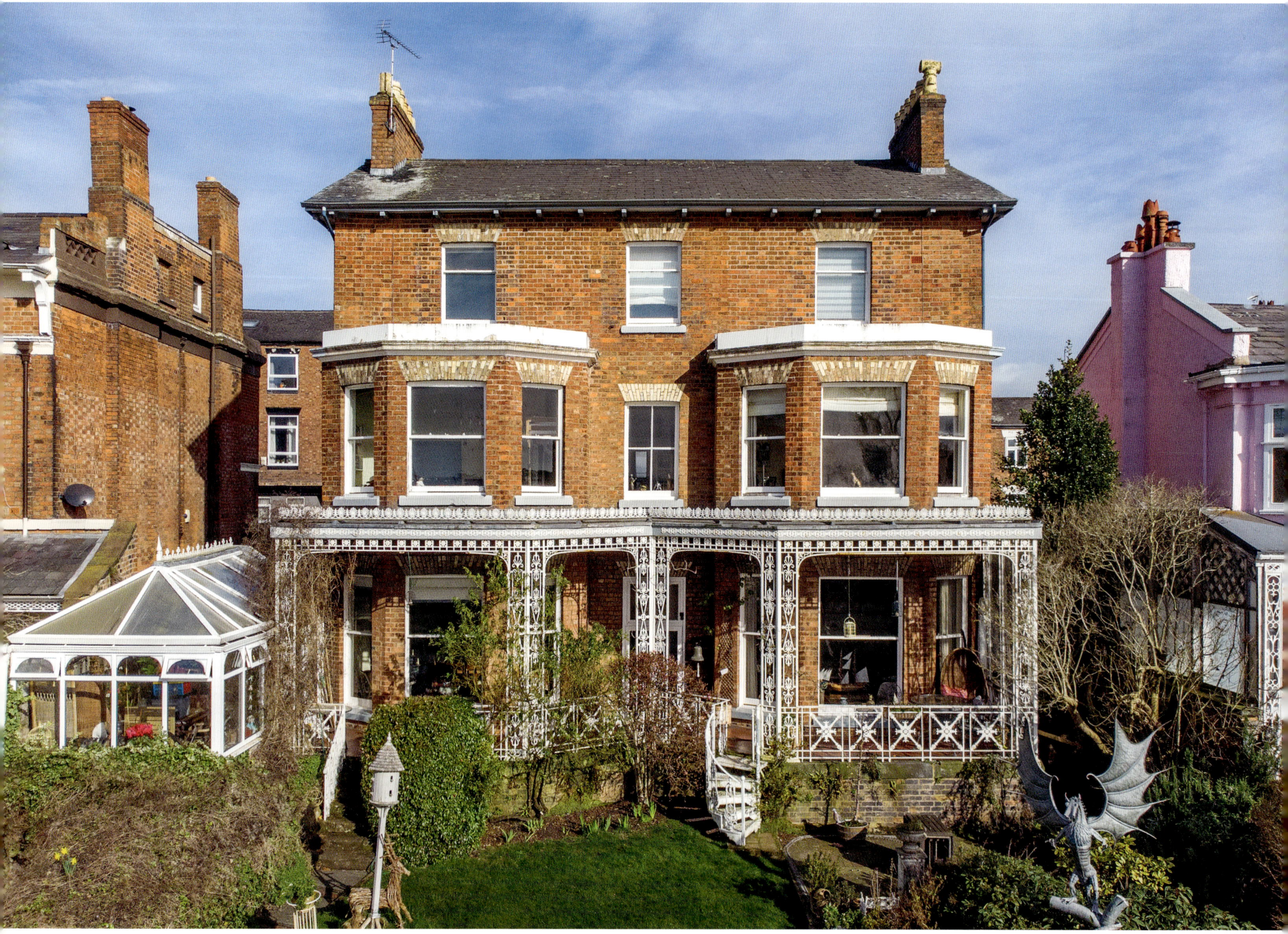

| CAERLLEON |

A timeless home
in the City of the Legions...

Conjuring Arthurian legend in its very title, Caerlleon, 'City of the Legions', is a home where history, mythology, magic and fantasy combine, resulting in a one-of-a-kind home, whose distinctiveness is beyond compare.

A little bit classical, a little bit medieval, Caerlleon might have been plucked from Frances Hodgson Burnett's 'The Secret Garden' or happened upon through a snowy woodland-wardrobe in Narnia. Once owned by Chester's 19th century railway engineer Thomas Brassey, Caerlleon's current vibes are as much classical or medieval as they are Victorian.

Step down into the entrance hall and through the looking glass into a world woven from the personalities of Caerlleon's loving owners. Minton tiles underfoot were the first of many treasures in this home to be uncovered 20 years ago. Broad, panelled doors, set within embellished architraves, beckon left and right, whilst beyond an archway ahead, an austere staircase curves elegantly up. Precursors of the thrills in store – neoclassical stone statues, wrought iron lighting, polished grandfather clocks and armoires – mingle in eclectic accord.

CAERLLEON

Individual rooms tell the tale of Caerlleon's occupants; an illustrious naval career documented in the sigils from countless warships and submarines displayed upon the walls. Dine over a map of Middle Earth with a fire blazing in the hearth; this is a room seemingly designed for the sole purpose of savouring stories.

Also on this ground level, a drawing room bathed in light embraces a more traditional feel in keeping with its Victorian roots, ideal for Christmas morning. Original rustic floor retains a classic feel in the utility room, whilst entering the kitchen is akin to stepping into a time capsule.

Taken from the 1950s Ideal Home Exhibition the kitchen retains its decades old American gas cooker and curved cabinetry: 'We never felt the need to update it, it works so well'.

The journey through time and continents continues upstairs, where frescos handpainted by Oswestry-based artist Leo Donaghy depict scenes of family events. Caerlleon is a home that wears its story on its sleeve. Bathe in the revitalising waters of the Aegean, as the bathroom delivers you to Ancient Greece. Secret doors, staircases and screens imprinted with Alhambra scenes from the talented hand of maestro Donaghy transform Caerlleon into so much more than a house.

On route to the servants' quarters, catch a glimpse of Chester to the front, a surreal reminder of reality in a home in which you have already journeyed through Middle Earth and 1950s America to Ancient Greece.

Rooms devoted to the passions and pleasures of those residing within its embrace are what distinguish Caerlleon. From model railway rooms to the cinema room on the cellar level, where exposed sandstone and two original Victorian range cookers give a glimpse of yet another era.

Distinct spaces yet in perfect synchronicity with each other, dinner in the dining room is followed by movie night in the cinema room. Jacuzzi rooms, wine cellars and even a wet room cheekily adorned with a well-known scene from a Tuscan frieze, cast and recreated in the dead of night, add frivolity and opulence in equal measure.

Outside, on a winter's day, the cascading gardens of Caerlleon look lovingly unkempt and a little overgrown; much like the home itself. Nineteenth century wrought iron railings stand the test of time on the uppermost terrace, a Mediterranean-feel verandah festooned in vines. Each level leading down to the river is met with a different mood, again, a reflection of the rooms within Caerlleon. Viburnum and cherry trees, a pleached pear tree adored by birds, which visit the garden in constant succession. Wildlife is in abundance, a wily fox and even a fierce dragon spied in the grounds…

The river takes on a magical glint in light of a visit to Caerlleon: a home that would be wonderful anywhere, but for its elevation, gardens and riverside setting becomes simply magical.

| 25 UNIQUE HOMES OF CHESTER |

STRETTON HALL

Pride and Prejudice Prestige…

Straight out of a Jane Austen novel, Stretton Hall displays its handsome Georgian symmetry, proud as a peacock. With its unusual Flemish brick and lime mortar façade, Stretton Hall's unique look is very much of its 1763 time.

Precision cropped box hedging to the front complements the formality of its appearance. Yet there is a tantalising warmth about the canted protrusion of the pretty pediment-topped front door, puffed out in pleasure within its central bay, arrived upon via an arc of double-sided steps.

A Grade-II listed home, Stretton Hall has been respectfully enhanced and recreated in traditional fashion; the imposing pillars of the entrance hall painted to match with the shades of the marble fireplace. Reaching up to the vaulted ceiling of the rear hall, pillars erected by previous occupants emulate their counterparts. Down in the sandstone cellar, an incredible vaulted ceiling features.

STRETTON HALL

Fireplaces and bathrooms are easily miscounted in a home of Stretton Hall's magnitude, but the fireplace in the 'pink' drawing room is impossible to miss, embellished with purple-blue bands of the rare semi-precious mineral Blue John.

While not every fireplace is original, all are in working order, providing warmth to a home that, in spite of its size, retains its welcome.

Alterations have respectfully been made to Stretton Hall; new wooden flooring, a staircase from the sitting room leading down to the garden, mirroring the entrance steps. Gentle additions to help daily life at Stretton Hall flow more smoothly; the bare bricks of a former orangery plastered to create a sitting room for comfortable entertaining, cupboards in the hallway aggrandised with mahogany doors and architraves. Traditional style radiators have been installed, with work undertaken to fix the shutters to the windows.

Windows are a key feature of Stretton Hall, framing impossibly picturesque views from almost every room. Venetian windows draw in an abundance of light, providing romantic vistas onto the topiary garden from the summer drawing room.

Revolve your day around the movement of the sun; with rooms recommending themselves for morning coffee, afternoon tea and supper according to the natural daylight. The Aga in the kitchen acts as a warm and homely axis.

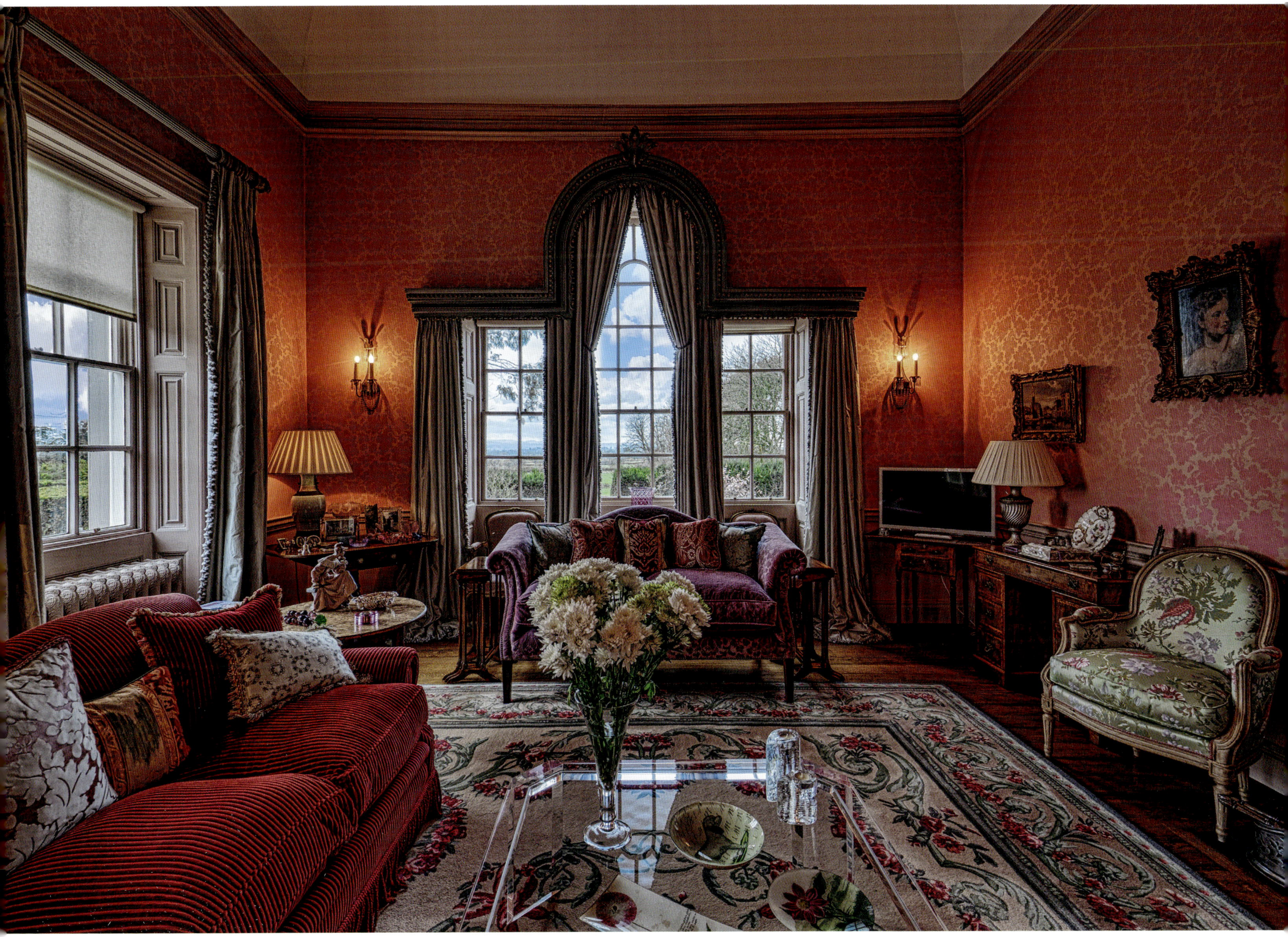

| 25 UNIQUE HOMES OF CHESTER |

STRETTON HALL

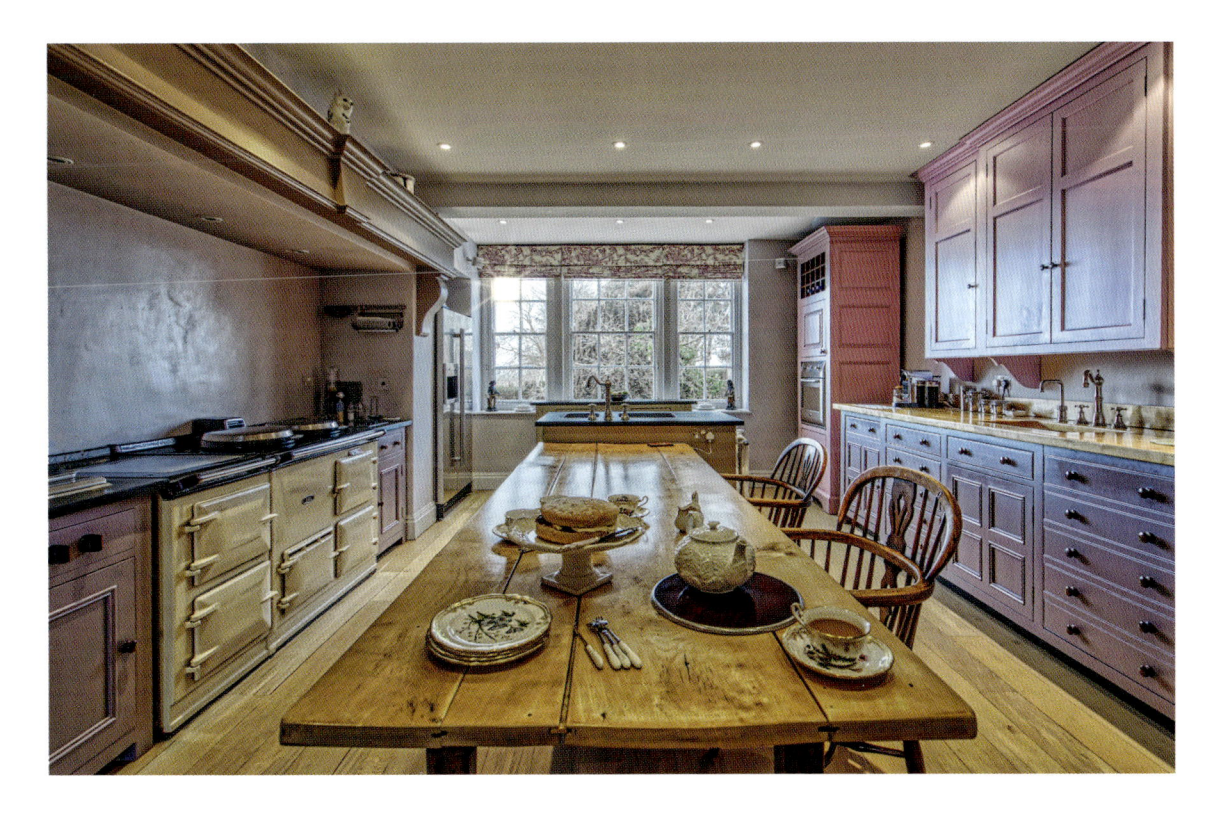

Expansive in its footprint, yet surprisingly intimate; individual rooms are light and bright, but not oversized, and the absence of large corridors means there is no sense of 'rattling around' Stretton Hall.

From the master bedroom, shuttered windows open to provide 'Downton Abbey' views of a majestic Cedar of Lebanon, an impressive sight to wake up to.

A home that brings pleasure to those who behold it, from invited guests to passing cyclists; Stretton Hall is admired by all.

Alive in the springtime, snowdrops, rhododendrons and daffodils carpet the grounds in colour. Verdant and voluminous gardens are subdivided for ease of

| STRETTON HALL |

communication when taking a stroll along the camelia walk, parkland, topiary or terrace gardens. The summer house garden, an Alice in Wonderland delight, is brimming with roses at the height of summer. From sunsets over the Welsh hills to unadulterated night skies sprinkled in starlight, Stretton Hall sparkles with equal brilliance outdoors as it does from within.

Of course, no one 'owns' Stretton Hall, there are simply custodians, honouring and appreciating its beauty, hoping that those who follow after will continue the tradition with as much love and care.

| 25 UNIQUE HOMES OF CHESTER |

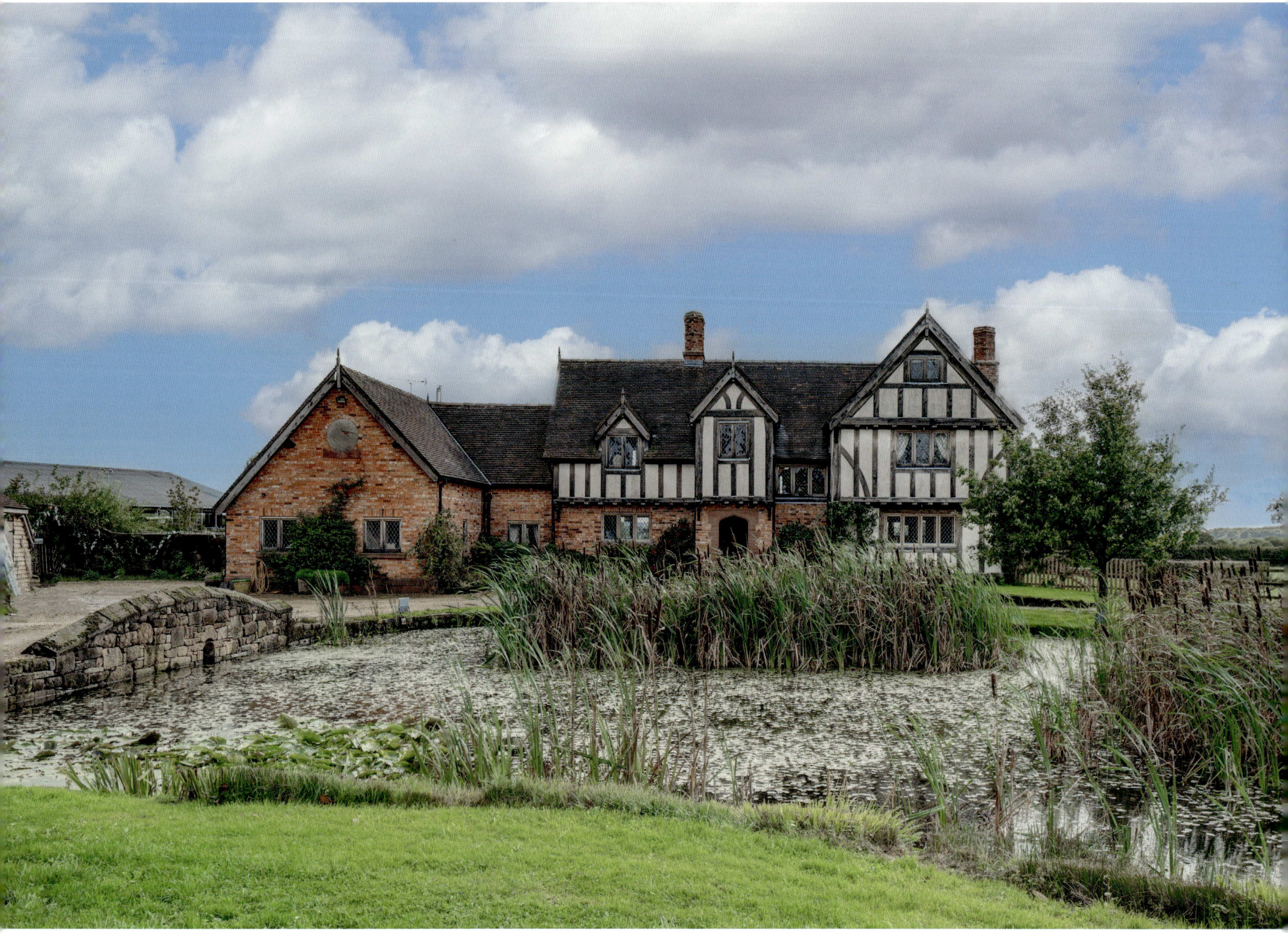

| HUNTINGTON HALL FARM |

A lifestyle home laced with understated luxury...

When searching for the perfect home, success doesn't always come easily. But for those who accomplish the often challenging task of designing and building their own home, the dream becomes reality.

Over a quaint bridge, at Huntington Hall Farm, the Tudoresque timber-frame, bespoke-built home stands handsomely beyond a large nature pond. Comfortable in its surrounds the design is respectful to the greenbelt land in which it resides. No square peg in a round hole, the timber frame home was designed specifically to accommodate the needs of the working farm within which it is set.

Affording a sense of separation from the day's toil, the home is offset from the working areas, from the cows, manège and stables. During and at the end of a busy day's work, the farmhouse stands as a sanctuary to return home to.

HUNTINGTON HALL FARM

First and foremost, Huntington Hall Farm is a lifestyle home. Unpretentious and welcoming, yet elegantly inviting in its decorative and technological subtleties. A home for children to enjoy as they grow up, where parties can be held without anxieties over spillages and mucky shoes. As such, practical tiled floors are easy to clean after a day on the farm, and easily wipeable after a night on the wine!

Each element has been carefully planned to fit with the flow of everyday life. From a farming perspective, the utility room is the perfect day-to-day entrance, returning home with muddy dogs and straw covered riding boots.

When welcoming guests, the entrance hall has wow factor prestige, serenaded in light from the huge floor to ceiling window, directing the eye upward to the showstopping galleried landing with its feature central light. At every angle, beams and timbers entreat the eye, adding picturesque interest and delight. Practicality and elegance go hand in hand without pretention at Huntington Hall Farm, where large slabs of tiling are suffused with warmth from contemporary underfloor heating. Upstairs, this modern touch is counterbalanced by cast iron radiators.

Classic décor furthers the traditional farmhouse feel, chic, timeless and understated. The comforts and conveniences of contemporary living are felt in the automated lighting touch screens, the integrated sound system in the sitting room, kitchen and formal dining room and data cables and computer points secreted throughout the home. Ancient in appearance only, this home is tuned in to present day needs and future proofed.

The hub of the home, the kitchen-living room flows onto the office, providing a sociable space for the family to congregate. Bifolding leaded doors open to frame pleasing sightlines along the pergola-covered gravel pathway where paddocks and fields and hillside views flow on from the garden. Warmed by the kitchen Aga and log burner, the substantial space is homely and welcoming.

Outside, a purpose-built pub in the garage serves as an extension of the indoor entertaining space, in a home whose primary purpose is providing pleasure and making memories for its family. Barbeques, hot tub parties or simply soaking up the sunshine are all in a day's work.

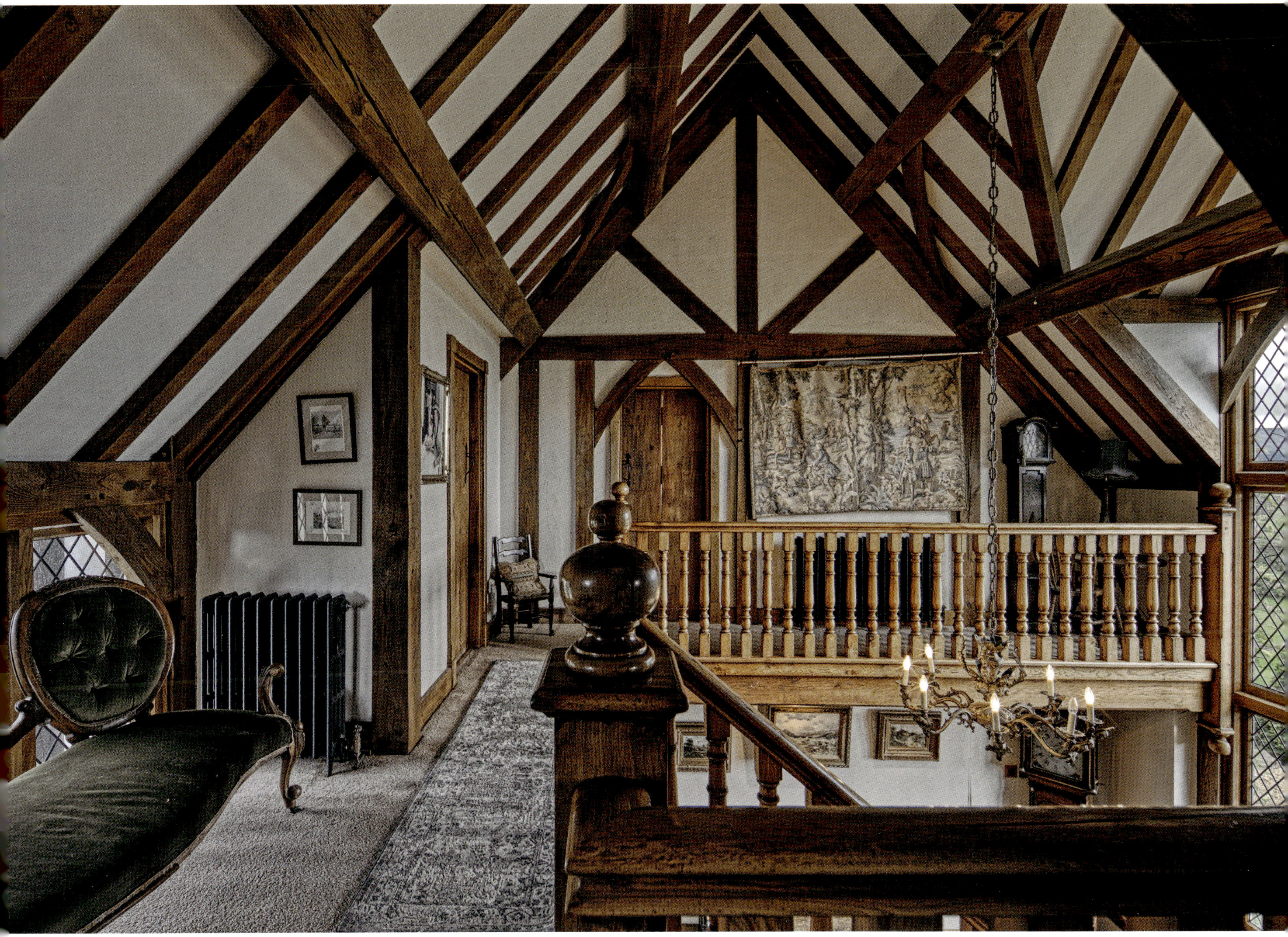

Formal entertaining is best enjoyed in the feasting hall dining room, distinguished by its exposed timbers, 'tree eating' centrepiece fireplace replete with large sandstone lintel, and commodious dining table seating up to twenty guests. Christmas dinner is something to be savoured and celebrated in style at Huntington Hall Farm.

Grand and spacious in its proportions, Huntington Hall Farm is not a home of echoing corridors and quiet rooms. A hive of activity, this is first and foremost a practical home, lived in all the time and filled with the comings and goings of family and friends. A comfort blanket of a home filled with fun, laughter and stories.

Entirely in keeping with the personality of its owners, Huntington Hall Farm is a comfortable and easy home, brimming with personality and laced with understated luxury.

| 25 UNIQUE HOMES OF CHESTER |

| HUNTINGTON HALL FARM |

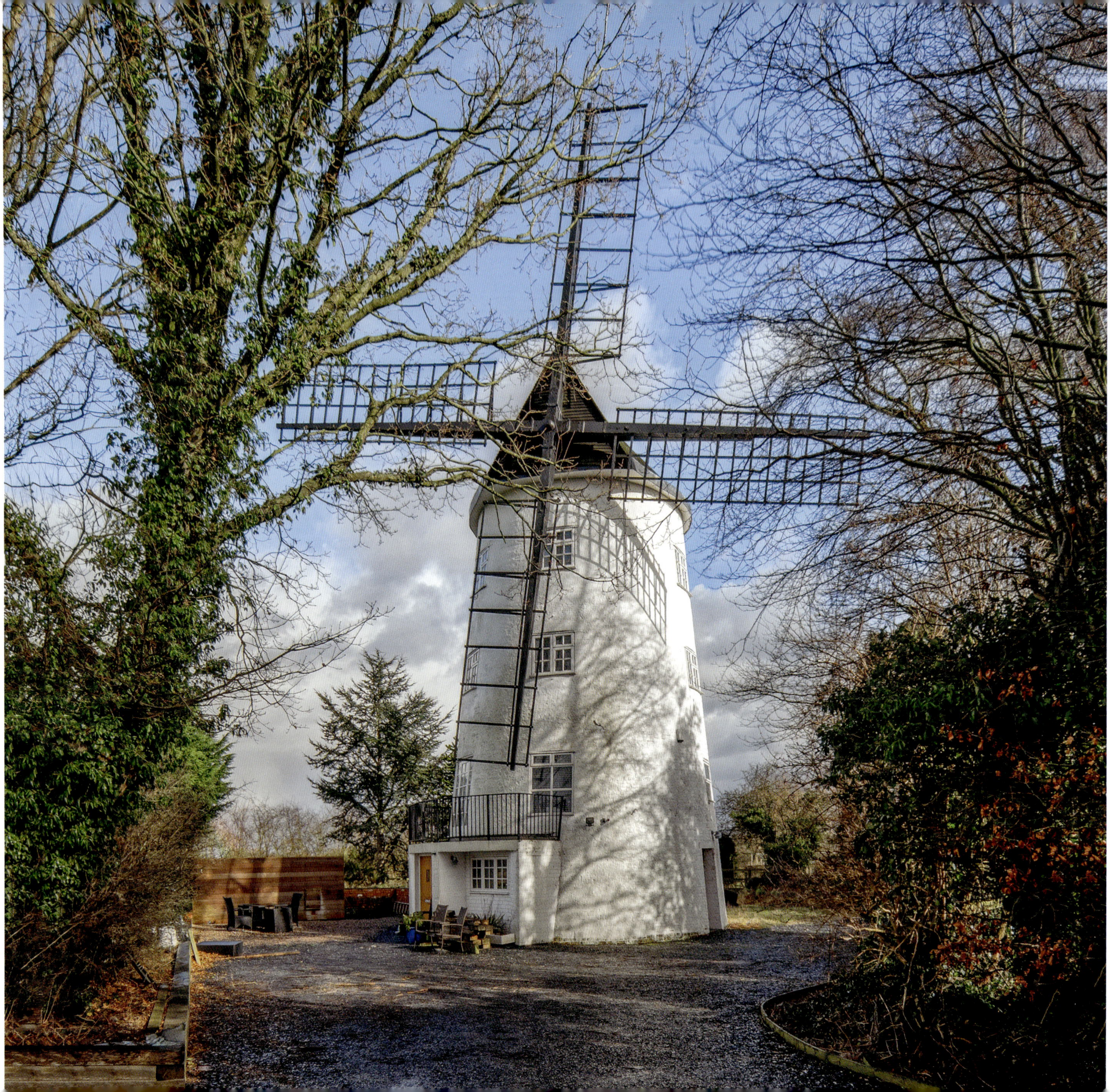

| GIBBET WINDMILL |

A romantic relic of bygone times...

Romantic remnants of a time gone by, in their dwindling numbers, England's windmills hold a childlike magic incomparable to all other structures.

Like a scene from Ian Fleming's Chitty Chitty Bang Bang, Gibbet Windmill evokes that whimsical nostalgia for the past. And just like the timeless 'fantasmagorical' children's tale, there is a tantalisingly dark side to Gibbet Windmill's past.

Originally built in 1610 to serve the nearby port of Shotwick, which at the time was more prominent than Liverpool, Gibbet Windmill's grisly moniker relates to a murder committed in the 1700s. According to legend, three Irish workers, having milled the grain, quarreled over how the money would be distributed, resulting in the murder of the older brother.

Following the fratricide, the two surviving brothers fled to the nearby Greyhound Inn in Saughall, confessing their crimes to a barmaid before attacking her. Found guilty of their crimes, in an age that pre-dated the police force, the pair were hanged for their heinous acts at Upton Barracks before

GIBBET WINDMILL

being strung up in gibbet chains outside the site of the crime, as per the custom of the times.

Gibbet Windmill continued milling up until 1920. Burned out following the second world war, this historic building was converted to residential use in the 1970s.

Purchased by its current owners in a dilapidated yet habitable condition a decade ago, the windmill has since been renovated from top to bottom, by one who passed by its sails as a child at the tender age of ten and made a vow to one day become its owner.

Rescued from the decay of time, among its many renovations and repairs are a new roof and sails, in full working order but set on a break for practicality. An old 70s-style extension has been dismantled with plans for a stunning side extension in place and due to be carried out in the near future.

Cool in summer, warm in winter, the conical nature of Gibbet Windmill makes for a constant battle with the elements, requiring diligent attention. Shot blasted back to brick, its render stripped, ('the render just brought in more water') Gibbet Windmill stands freshly painted and sealed, ready to brace against the weather.

Inside, rigid steel joists lend an industrial air to the windmill. Precision-perfect spiral stairs once belonging to prominent Birkenhead shipbuilders Cammel Laird run right the way up through the centre, purchased from a salvage museum to fit to each level exactly.

Quirks of design pay homage to the whimsy of life within the walls of a windmill; in the kitchen reclaimed oak carvings of Yorkshire furniture maker Robert 'Mouseman' Thomas have been worked into the woodwork of the ceilings.

Wind your way to the top of the windmill to arrive at the most unique bedroom, evocative of modern American lofts with its triple height vaulted ceiling. In the cone of the roof itself, with all the windings from the workings of the sails on prominent display, it is an incredible space in which to be as the wind drives up the estuary.

Once a working mill, there is no attempt to enforce minimalist modernity on this home, which stands firm to its roots. At one with the landscape, it sits with an ancient oak tree in an acre of field, a homing beacon for flocks of geese, who swoop round it nightly before settling down to roost on the marshes. Nature's own chronometer, it is impossible to imagine a time when this retro cool iconic landmark will cease to stand.

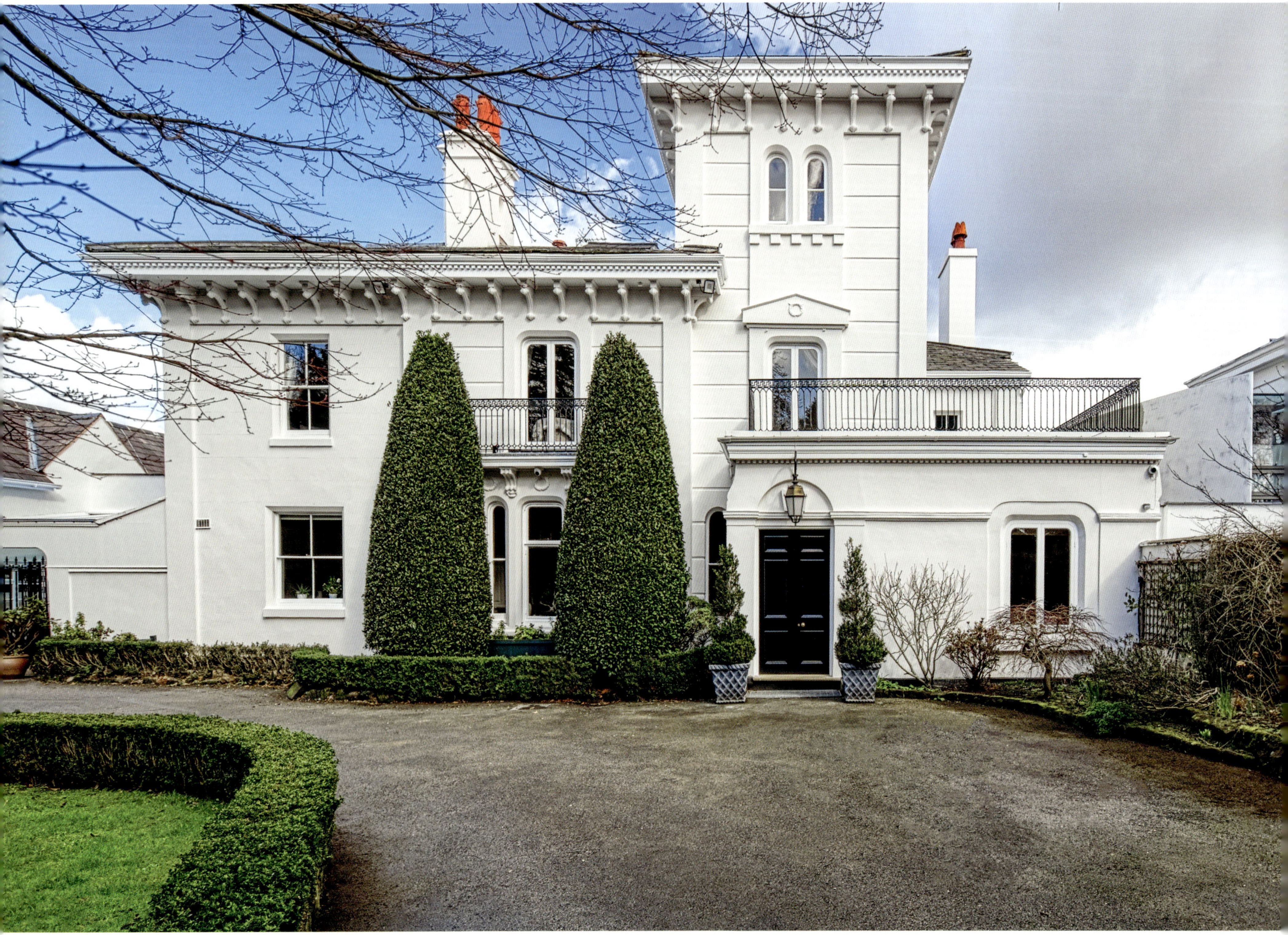

| TOWER HOUSE |

Italian elegance
overlooking the River Dee...

Welcome to prestigious Curzon Park, an exclusive residential neighbourhood of characterful homes, dating back to the 19th century. Lying along the verdant shores of the River Dee, it was developed by Richard Curzon-Howe, the 1st Earl Howe.

Only a ten-minute stroll from Chester and counting among its treasures views out to the iconic Grosvenor Bridge and Chester Racecourse, Tower House is perhaps one of the most visually striking of them all.

Italianate in its design, ornate corbels, bold boxed eaves and a pronounced wrought iron balcony make for an impactful first impression; one that fits perfectly with the Roman history of Chester, its historic walls, black and white buildings and bridges.

Formerly owned by MBNA, this Grade-II listed home continues the theme of Italian opulence both inside and out. Beyond the grand front door, detailed plaster coving embellishes the ceiling like tiers on a wedding cake. Arched transoms and windows deliver light throughout. Décor combines refined

TOWER HOUSE

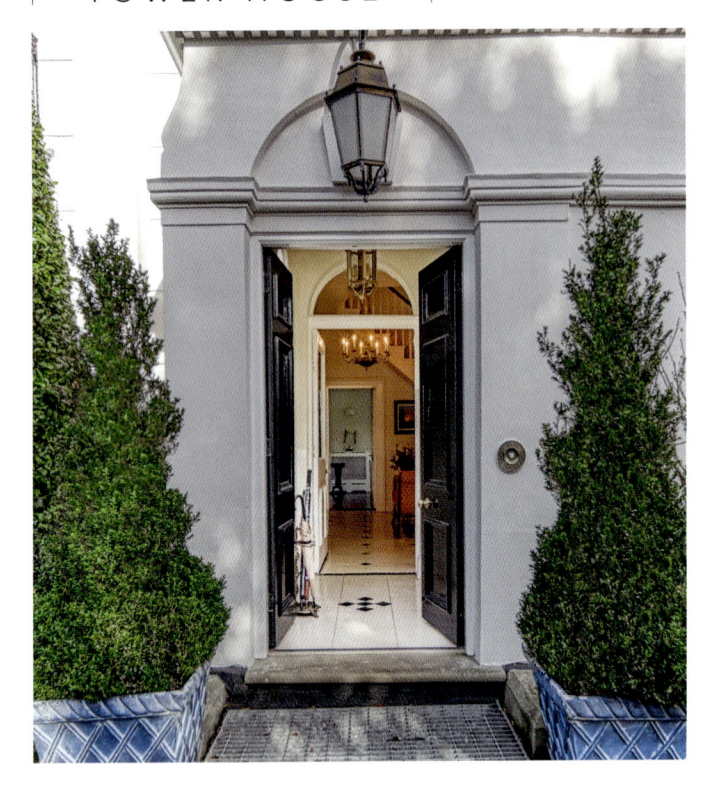

traditional taste and heritage tones with a colourful display of art, both modern and classical.

An all-season home, the open fireplace in its marble Victorian surround burns bright in winter, providing a warm welcome in the lounge. Archways and bay windows constantly draw the eye to new rooms, and winning views out over the river to the Racecourse.

Entertaining at Tower House is an obligatory pleasure, the kitchen cleverly divided by a broad chimney breast to accommodate both dining and preparation spaces; sociable yet separate.

Pockets of privacy can be found throughout, none more romantic than the tower office, nestled at the top of a staircase, hidden away for total tranquility.

| 25 UNIQUE HOMES OF CHESTER |

| 25 UNIQUE HOMES OF CHESTER |

| TOWER HOUSE |

Glowing sunrises and rosy sunsets are best enjoyed from the bedroom terrace, or outdoors on the stone terrace, which once housed a swimming pool. Accessible from every room on the ground floor, the views are enhanced by the fresh air.

Terraced, landscaped gardens are mature in their established planting and alive with colour in springtime. Box hedging and imposing stone planters and fountains formalise the Italianate feel outdoors.

A one-off home, rich in both design and history, warm and welcoming in spite of its grandeur, Tower House embodies a sense of belonging, of arrival. Like all homes of its calibre and vintage, it demands a little love in return; love that is freely given for a home of such prestige

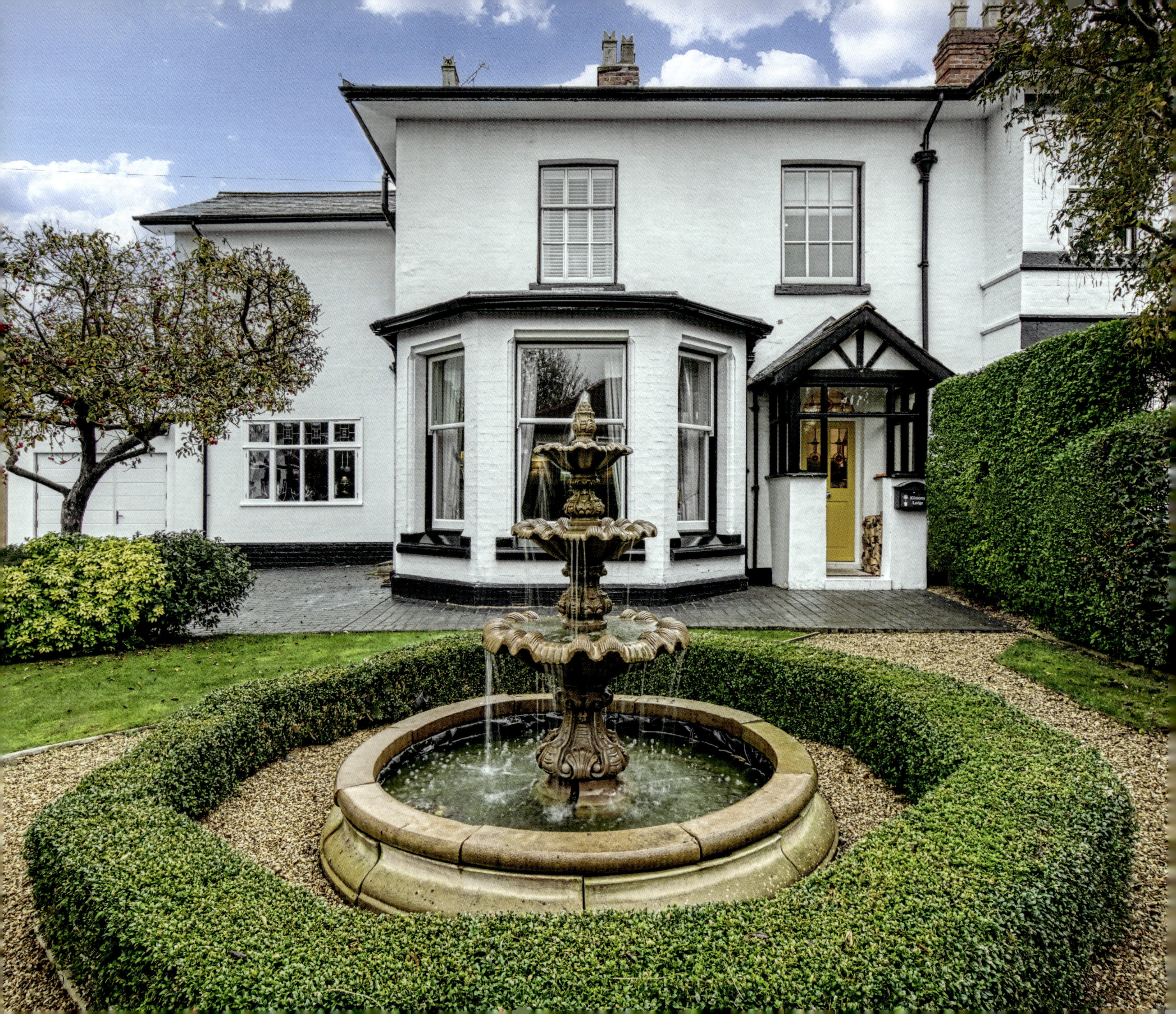

KILMOREY LODGE

Love's labours won...

Hidden away behind high hedges, discovering Kilmorey Lodge, a Georgian gem amongst a peppering of post war properties, is like stepping through a portal to another plane.

Easy to miss amidst this alien landscape, yet once seen, never forgotten, Kilmorey Lodge is a home steeped in history; well-loved and well-lived in by all who have dwelt within its walls (including prominent Chester family Dixons, of Dixons Seeds of Chester fame).

Originally one with the attached neighbour, Kilmorey Lodge was known as Springfield House, its modern title taken from the Earl of Kilmorey, owner of the surrounding land. Dating back to 1831, it both pre- and post-dates the railway which once ran close by.

Kilmorey Lodge is a home capable of withstanding the test of time, yet also a home that moves with the times, its stature ebbing and flowing over the ages. Purchased in 1929 by lauded Chester builder Thomas Warrington, an extension saw the addition of the current dining room and a bedroom.

KILMOREY LODGE

What was formerly the rear of the home now serves as the front, and where horse and carriage once swept up to an archway entrance, stands a private paved driveway. Georgian formality prevails to the front in a circular fountain feature.

Transformed from front to back, inside and out over decades, renovations retain a sympathetic nod to its Georgian heritage, whilst nurturing and cajoling the home into the 21st century.

Stained-glass windows in the dining room, diligently replaced with double glazing incorporating the original single 1929 panels, are an example of countless laborious efforts undertaken to pay homage to the original styling of the home. From reinstated Georgian panelling, to complementary specialist plaster cornicing in the hallway; to the meticulous job of stripping back mouldings in the lounge to rediscover the finesse and definition of its features, lost beneath countless coats of paint over the centuries; no detail is overlooked.

An endeavour not for the faint hearted, attention to detail in the restoration and reinvention of Kilmorey Lodge saw the challenge of sourcing Canadian pine (no longer imported) to complete the flooring in the entrance hall. Anachronisms of décor bear witness to the alterations of the years, with 'borrowed' Art Deco architraves embellishing the older lounge and floral cornerstones set within the doorway of the more recently built dining room.

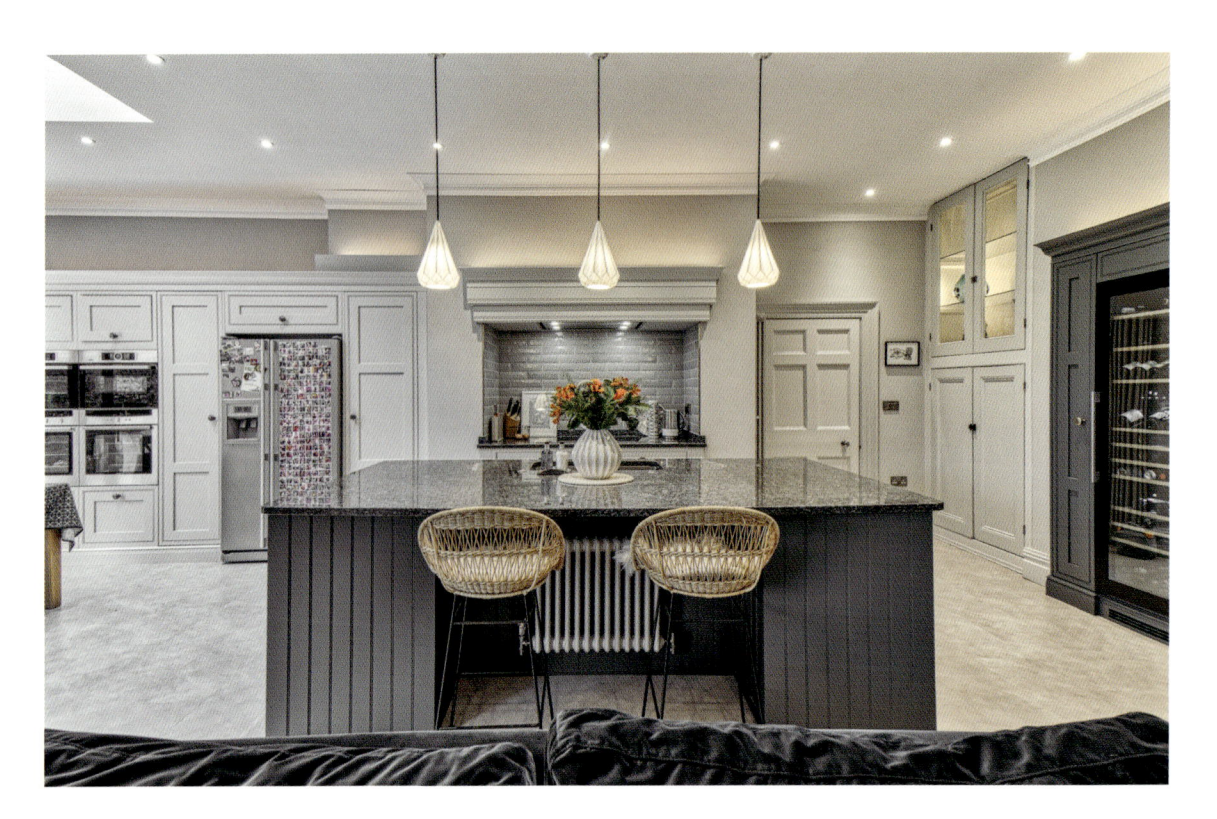

A legacy home, signifiers throughout provide a glimpse of the past; fireplaces in stone cellars with markers reading 'sugar' and 'salt'; original frieze work in the kitchen bestowing a Regency feel; bountiful bedrooms; dumb waiter shafts; broad doorways and a secret, stained-glass topped panel door revealing a hidden laundry room.

Beyond the kitchen, 'The Den' provides an indoor-outdoor, sheltered entertaining space in which to eat, drink and be merry whatever the weather. Mediterranean planting evokes a calm and relaxing mood, whilst an illuminated water feature nods to the 'spring' at the heart of the original home. A cedar outdoor kitchen area enables the lush gardens to be appreciated throughout the seasons.

Conviviality and congregation are at the heart of Kilmorey Lodge, a home that craves clamour, camaraderie and companionship. A home that beats with the heart and soul poured into preserving it for the future. A continued labour of love and true family home.

| 25 UNIQUE HOMES OF CHESTER |

MANOR HOUSE

To the Manor born...

Born on the cusp of transitioning architectural styles, Georgian symmetry meets with Victorian gothic gables at Manor House, on Queen's Park Road. A most unique and elegant home.

The Manor House borrows architectural traits from both the Georgian and Victorian eras resulting in a harmonious blend of features and quirks which could be said to transcend both periods.

Situated only a ten-minute stroll across the suspension bridge to the shops, restaurants and culture of Chester, Manor House is also only a short drive from open countryside and the beautiful Welsh hills; a home characterised by balance - a pivotal point in both geography and history.

Untouched for many years, this former eight-bedroom bed and breakfast establishment features in posters found in the local visitor centre, depicting the area in the 1850s before the development of homes along the river, testament to Manor House's longevity.

| MANOR HOUSE |

During the 22-year tenure of its current owners, Manor House has undergone a renaissance. Blocked fireplaces have been reinstated, including original Range ovens in both the kitchen and morning room. With original coving, ceiling friezes and fireplaces in situ, Manor House was restored to its former glory.

The easy, flowing feel of Manor House is evident upon arrival into the broad entrance hall, embellished by original stained glass and stone quoin windows, where the elegant staircase sweeps up ahead, light filtering down from the atrium ceiling above. Centred around the hall, Georgian symmetry connects spaces, drawing people together. Consequently, Manor House is a home at home when entertaining; its doors and arms open to all.

Interesting features are found throughout, from the unusual Arts and Crafts style window above the fireplace in the living room, to the high skirtings, intricate plaster mouldings and working shutters found throughout the reception rooms. The morning room, elevated from its former role as scullery, now connects to the topiary gardens through French double doors. Modern enhancements such as this and a newly fitted kitchen are the exception rather than the rule at Manor House, respectfully undertaken and balanced by painstaking renovation work uncovering quarry tiled flooring and the re-enamelling of the original Range shines out anew, with the addition of Fired Earth Dutch tiles a sympathetic touch.

True to its heritage, yet not preserved in the past, Manor House yields happily to serve the needs of those within its embrace. Bedrooms are repurposed

| 25 UNIQUE HOMES OF CHESTER |

| 25 UNIQUE HOMES OF CHESTER |

| MANOR HOUSE |

as media rooms, studies and yoga studios. Eclectic décor complements the home; boudoirs enhanced by evocative pillared fireplaces and de Gournay hand painted wall hangings telling tales of travel from west to east and back again.

Southwest facing, the private garden was landscaped in 2008 to include topiary and espalier planting, with curved hornbeams and mature yew hedging creating a formal feel. In perfect view of the morning room an imported Italian white camelia heralds the arrival of spring beside a lionhead water feature and box hedging.

The elegance of Manor House is enriched by its warmth, cosseting those who enter in its convivial embrace. Cherished by its owners, through their respectful preservation of its unique features, the home seems to extend the same courteous welcome.

| 25 UNIQUE HOMES OF CHESTER |

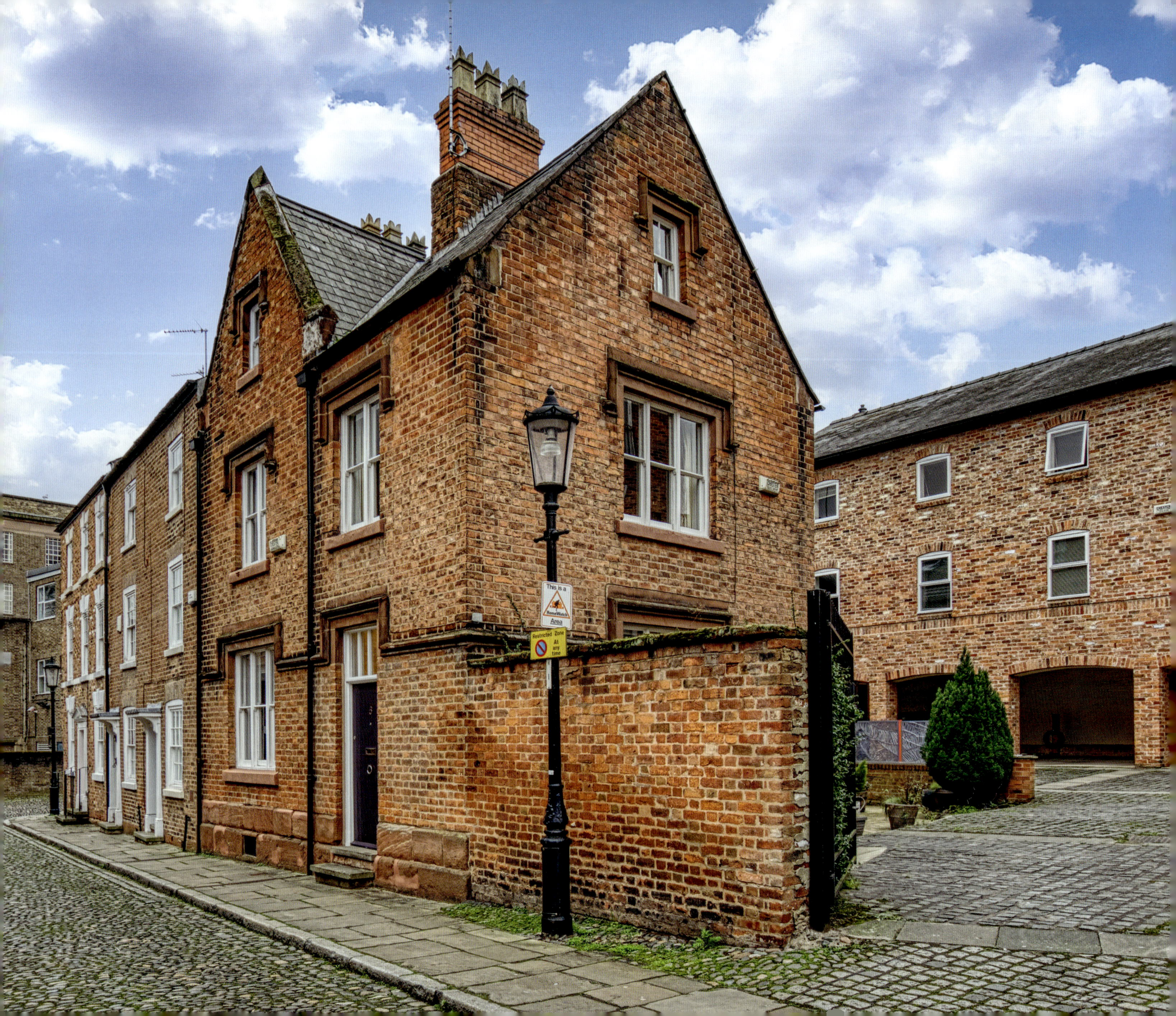
This is a
HomeWatch
Area
Restricted Zone
At any time

| SHIPGATE |

A flighty Victorian
with a mid-century taste...

Kitsch, flighty and frivolously fun, with not a right angle in sight; six years of love and labour has brought Shipgate, a Victorian town house with a vibrant past, out of the doldrums.

Out with the Artex and the terracotta and mint green 'serviceable' carpets and in with freshly skimmed walls, engineered French oak flooring and crisp, invigorating Little Greene colours. Shipgate, once again, stands in shipshape condition.

A home with strong merchant connections, right in the centre of Chester only a few paces from the river, stepping along the cobbled street to reach Shipgate is akin to stepping back in time. Built in around 1840 upon the footprint of a former inn, ancient carvings in the cellar depict the chosen vessels of those signing up for passage on ships. Images of a rosebud and a fish of some sort are evocative, tangible links to the past. Surprisingly comfortable, this bone-dry cellar now serves as a laundry and office. The working hub of the home.

Saved from imminent destruction in the 1970s through timely intervention from the Civic Trust, Michael Heseltine and the Home Office, a Shipgate plundered and pillaged of its timbers, fireplaces and original doors was sold for a pound.

SHIPGATE

Surprisingly bright for a period home, located on the corner, light is integral to Shipgate's warmth and welcome. Feature stained glass, a 1980s addition, adds an ethereal underwater feel to the entertaining spaces of the kitchen and dining room.

Brilliantly bold in its décor, the dining room is a beguiling space, designed for opulent dinner parties with the blinds closed and candles lit; a space to behold and in which to be beheld. A flighty Victorian with a mid-century taste.

Grade II listed, naturally, a unique bread oven in the kitchen is subject to a separate conservation order, providing a flashback to the days when homes without ovens would take the Sunday joint to pubs and bakeries for roasting. Now a modern kitchen, yet not to the detriment of character; wood rather than granite takes a softer approach to epicurean progress.

Providing plenty of space for separation whilst at once retaining perfect party flow, each of the four levels offers a destination in itself. Sample the quiet sanctuary of the snug, an intimate and light space with disco vibes, whose bespoke blinds were commissioned from an 18th Century Wedgewood design, briefly licensed for reproduction at great cost.

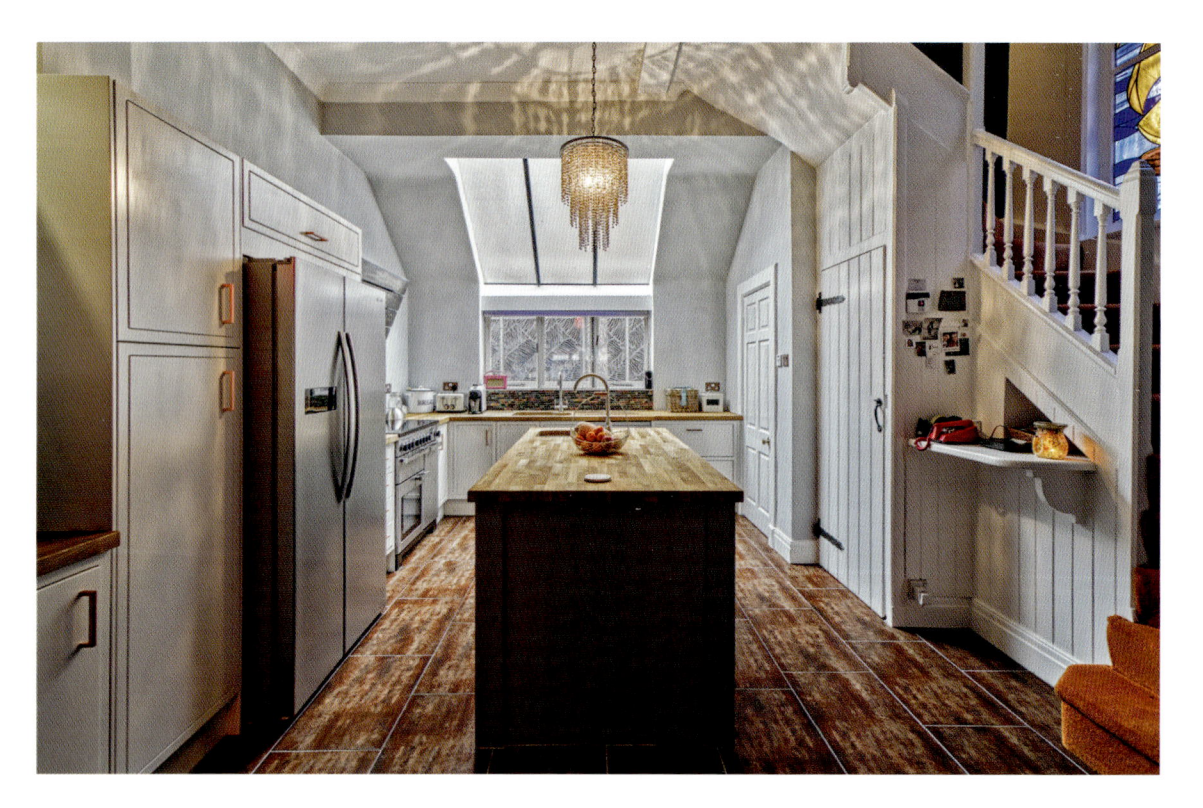

On the first floor, the drawing room is set behind an enormous doorway built to accommodate the burgeoning bustles of the Victorian era. A room with a soporific effect, peaceful, quiet and awash with light and Little Greene's soothing Slaked Lime, sense the slight lilt of the floor and asymmetry of the walls : 'I think every room needs five per cent ugliness, because life is like that'. Imperfection is perfected in the old Sunday school cabinet, its tactile scorch mark casually covered by a drinks tray, adding warmth as the dropped candle would once have done. 'A little bit of something old and something gaudy', each room is gifted a touch of imperfection to make it homely, putting guests at ease.

Bedrooms over the top two floors display this formula, chandeliers, old trunks, deep windows and ornamental fireplaces. The uppermost floor becomes its own suite. Bedroom, dressing room, study and perhaps the most beautiful fireplace of all. Cubbyholes and alcoves, visions of maids or maiden aunts warming themselves, once upon a time, up high in the servants' quarters.

Outside, a secret suntrap on the cobbles serves up a dining area that is miniature yet mighty. Of course, the river with its lure of ice cream and coffee is less than five minutes' walk away in a city that, like Shipgate itself, seems to evolve and improve all the time.

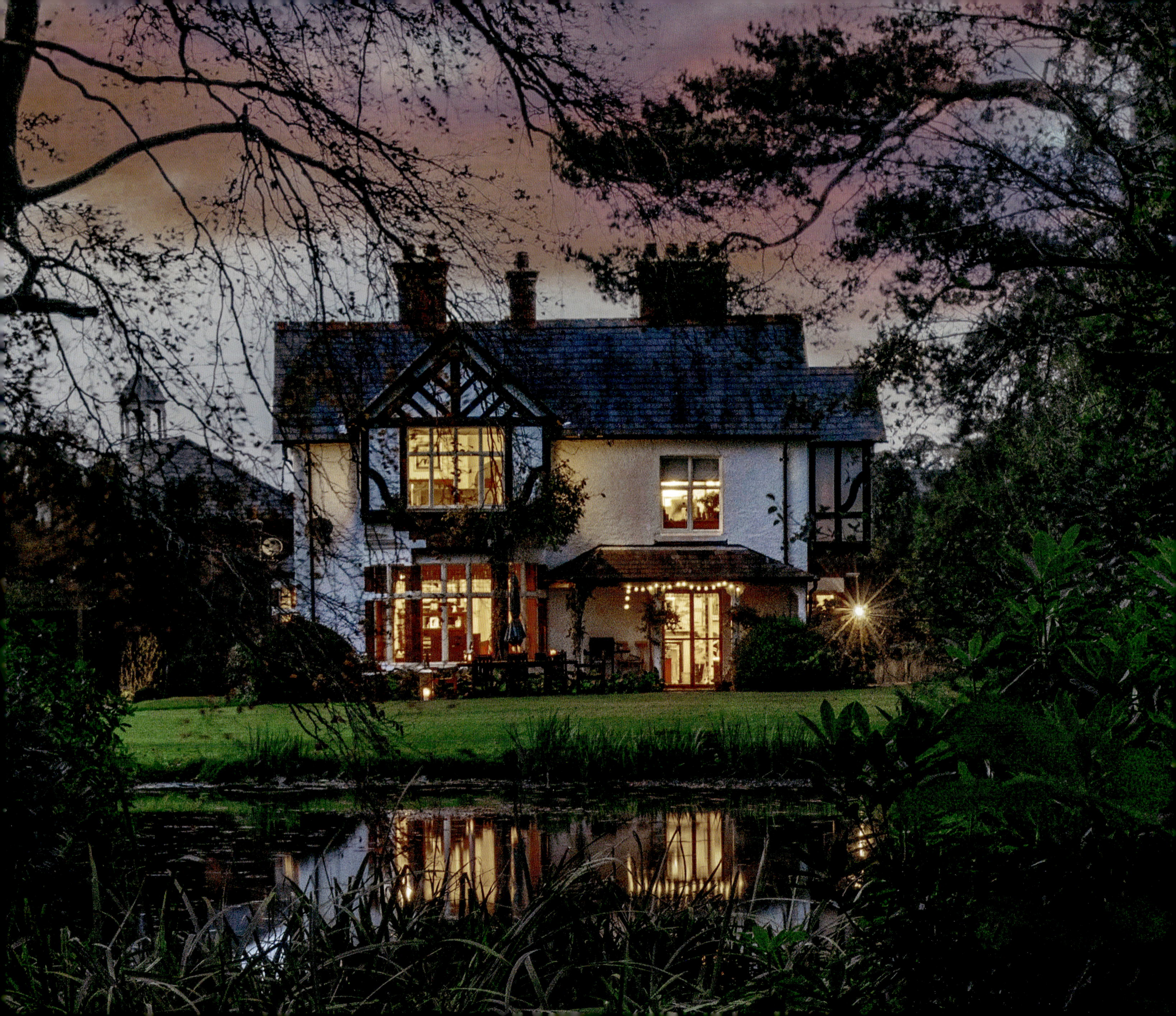

| THE CLOCK HOUSE |

Turning back the clock...

Dating back to the 1870s, The Clock House on the outskirts of the Cheshire village of Malpas, is a hidden countryside gem.

Wrapped up in 18 acres of land (and a lake), The Clock House is an unspoiled page in the region's rich history, with connections to prestigious local families including Chester's premier civil engineer Thomas Brassey. Born in nearby Buerton, Brassey was at the forefront of railway building across the globe during the 1800s.

Escaping the 'rip and replace' attitudes of the 1980s, The Clock House is a treasure trove of untouched, period delights, from its solid oak front door, feature stained-glass to the vintage black and red quarry tiled kitchen floor. However, it is the handsome wood panelled entrance hall and staircase that is cause for gasps of delight.

The Clock House is a pass-the-parcel collection of uniquely styled rooms, each with its own prize; from the lake views bestowed through the enormous stone mullion windows of the main drawing room, to the classic house pantry in the homely kitchen. Surprises lie in store in the boot room, where beneath

THE CLOCK HOUSE

a stone slab a barrel-vaulted cellar is preserved. An original pump is retained in the boiler house, whilst in the family room the original cast iron Range cooker sits within its original tiling.

Modern touches go hand in hand with the ancient; an enclosed swimming pool sits within a private walled garden, replete with its own kitchen, showering and changing facilities.

Stretching out for acres, it is the privacy and self-contained ease afforded by life at The Clock House which encapsulate its spirit. Games of croquet on the old grass tennis court, wanderings through the orchard, fields and woodland and on through a kissing gate and into the village of Malpas. Freshwater swimming can also be dipped into in the lake, with a boat house, duck house and an abundance of water lilies, irises and freshwater fish. Specimen trees surround, alongside a more formal rhododendron walk and structured rose pergola.

Amongst the outbuildings is the glorious Grade-II listed Carriage House, still retaining its original stabling, manger and broad wooden doors. Ostlers' accommodation above is evocative of the old mail route between Marble Arch, London and Birkenhead, running along what is now the A41.

Preserving the period perfectly is the original clock and bell, made by J B Joyce (who seek to claim to be the oldest clockmakers in the world, established in the 1600s); horologist behind the Eastgate Clock in Chester and the clock at Carnforth Railway Station, immortalised in the 1940s film Brief Encounter.

| 25 UNIQUE HOMES OF CHESTER |

| 25 UNIQUE HOMES OF CHESTER |

THE CLOCK HOUSE

A home of many parts, The Clock House is truly a lifestyle house. A miniature estate, brought to its fullest life when filled with the resounding laughter of families and friends. A gracious home whose character and grand rooms lend themselves to merriment and where, in good company, time ceases to exist.

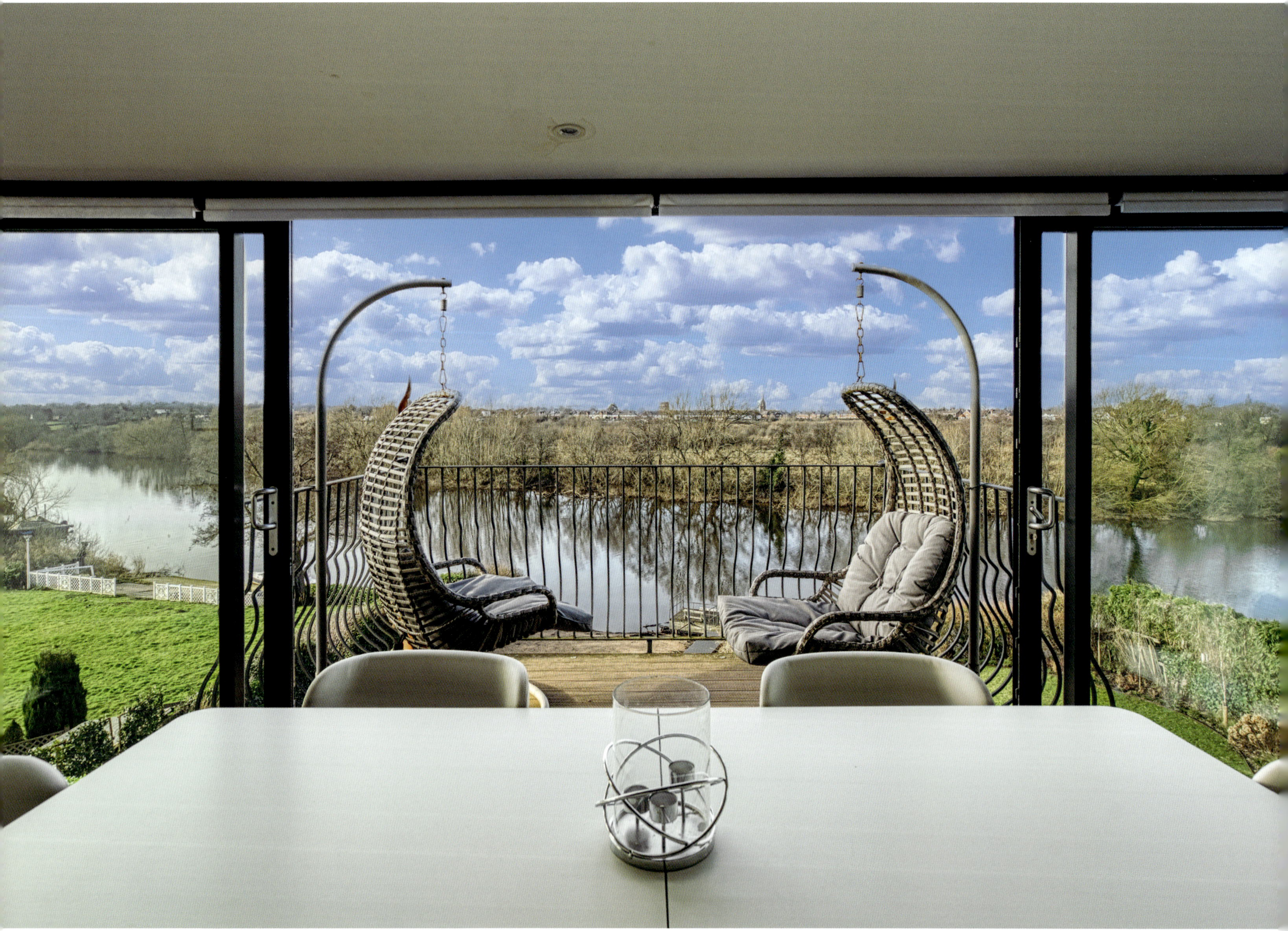

| WATERS EDGE |

A view with a home...

A home that is the sum of its parts, originally built in 1940, Waters Edge has metamorphosed many times over the decades. Having experienced no less than five extensions, its more recent transformation sought to improve rather than expand, removing walls and repositioning staircases in order to open up spaces and introduce a flow more in harmony with the river beside which it is set.

Magic always requires an exchange, and perhaps the magic of this home transformation is the inspiration it has taken not only from its surroundings but also from the experience of those undertaking the renovations. Embodying the easy flow of New York Colonial living, rooms connect seamlessly, designed to accommodate individual lifestyles within eyeshot of one another.

Stepping through the front door, the home – resplendent though it is - is rendered almost immaterial: it is the river, captured through a wall of sliding glass, that captivates.

With all the expectations of a 'normal house' from the approach, Waters Edge opens up like a lotus flower, entreating you through to its different colourful levels. On the entrance level, the kitchen is designed around the landscape, with aluminium sliding doors and balconies being but one connection to the flow of water beyond. Defined by a circular wave, the tile of the kitchen

WATERS EDGE

floor arcs into the wooden expanse beyond. Linked by both shape and colour, the shades of the surroundings to Waters Edge are drawn in through decorative tributes, such as the commissioned painting in the lounge downstairs; an artistic impression of a view from the pontoon looking up river; a kaleidoscope of colour, reflections of the sky.

An eclectic marriage of contemporary and classic, minimalism is eschewed for a more manageable mixture of treasured items which serve to enhance the homeliness of Waters Edge.

Homeliness and welcome are at the heart of Waters Edge, a true family home with space for all – each level offering versatility and even a gym that can serve as a sixth bedroom at the drop of a hat. The Scandi-style dining room too is ready for company, its table extending to seat 20 with ease. Waters Edge is a home at its happiest when entertaining; replete with its own changing room for the hot tub.

The river is an ever-present draw, made all the more tangible by extensive landscaping of the gardens, which now flow down to the river's banks. A day in the gardens of Waters Edge is like taking a trip to the beach…pack a picnic and pop out on the kayaks, boat and paddleboards. Privacy comes replete with views, with space for badminton and croquet on the lawned level and an impressive kitchen and dining area with soft seating to the upper tier. Even in winter, the garden plays a key role, hosting Christmas Day drinks huddled beside the heaters.

Riverside life is a life lived amidst a community of likeminded people. Those who appreciate the privilege of owning one of only around 120 homes on the banks of the River Dee. Its own village almost, the sights of boats and faces passing by soon become familiar.

Peaceful and ruralesque, yet 15 minutes' walk into the city, Waters Edge affords no compromise, instead offering the completeness of countryside and city as one. Flexible, encompassing and family-orientated with a stylish flow. Waters Edge is a unique home, in a unique city.

| 25 UNIQUE HOMES OF CHESTER |

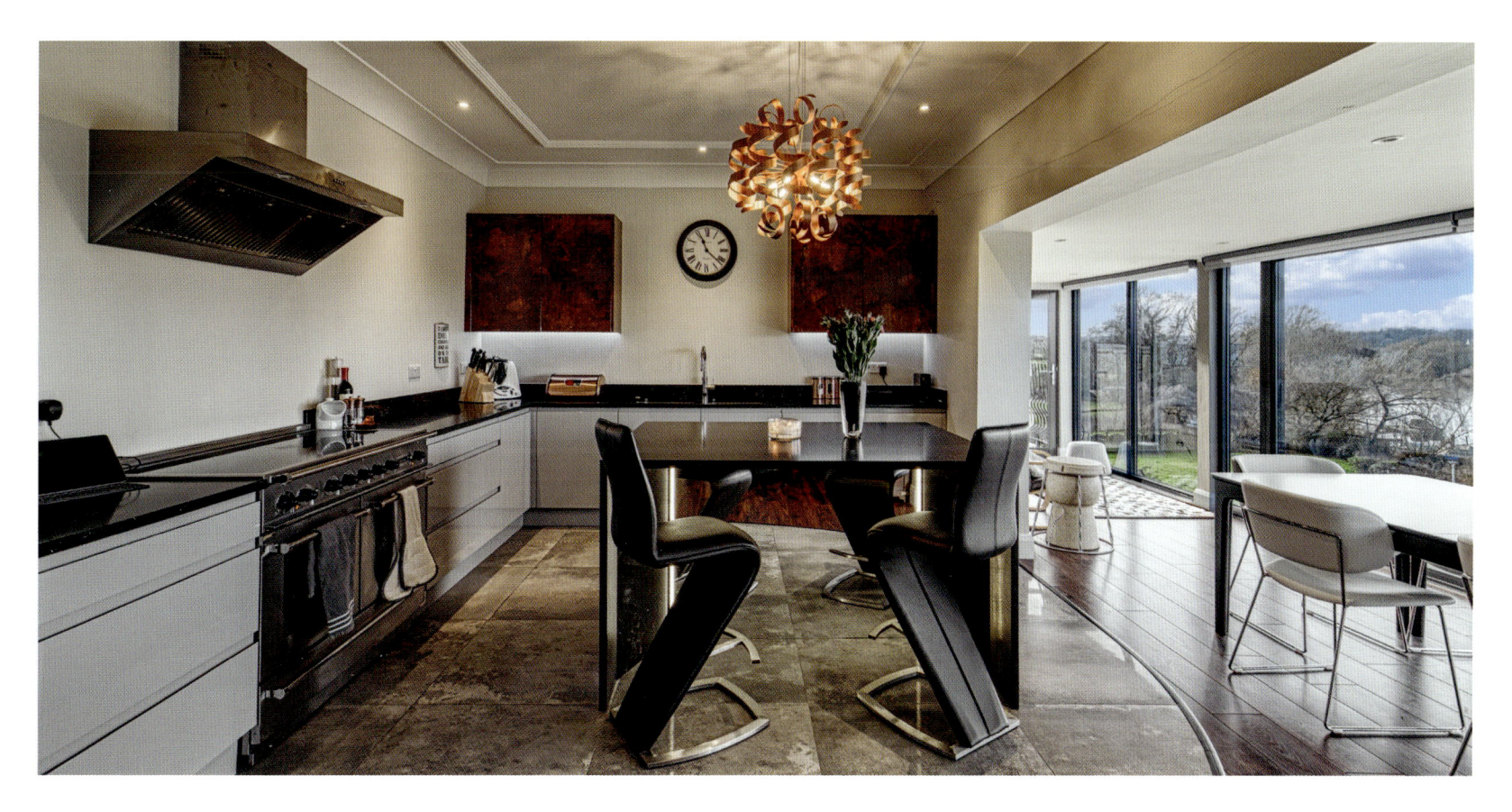

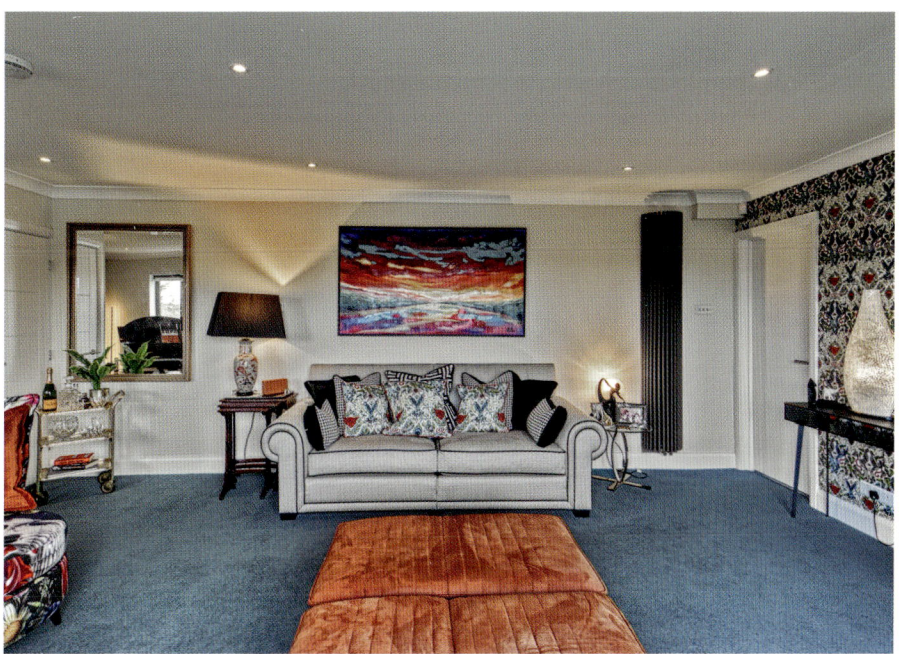

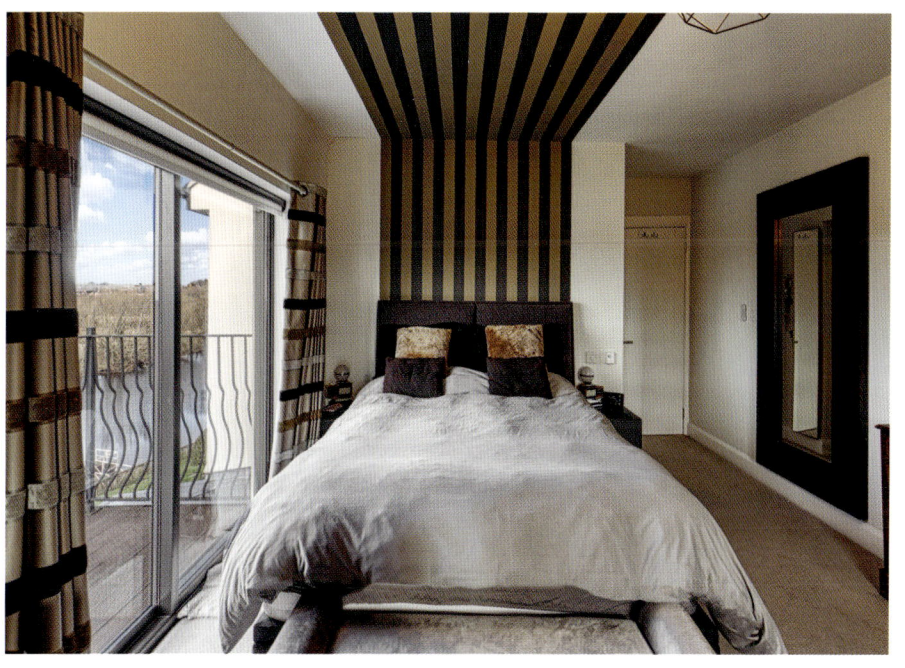

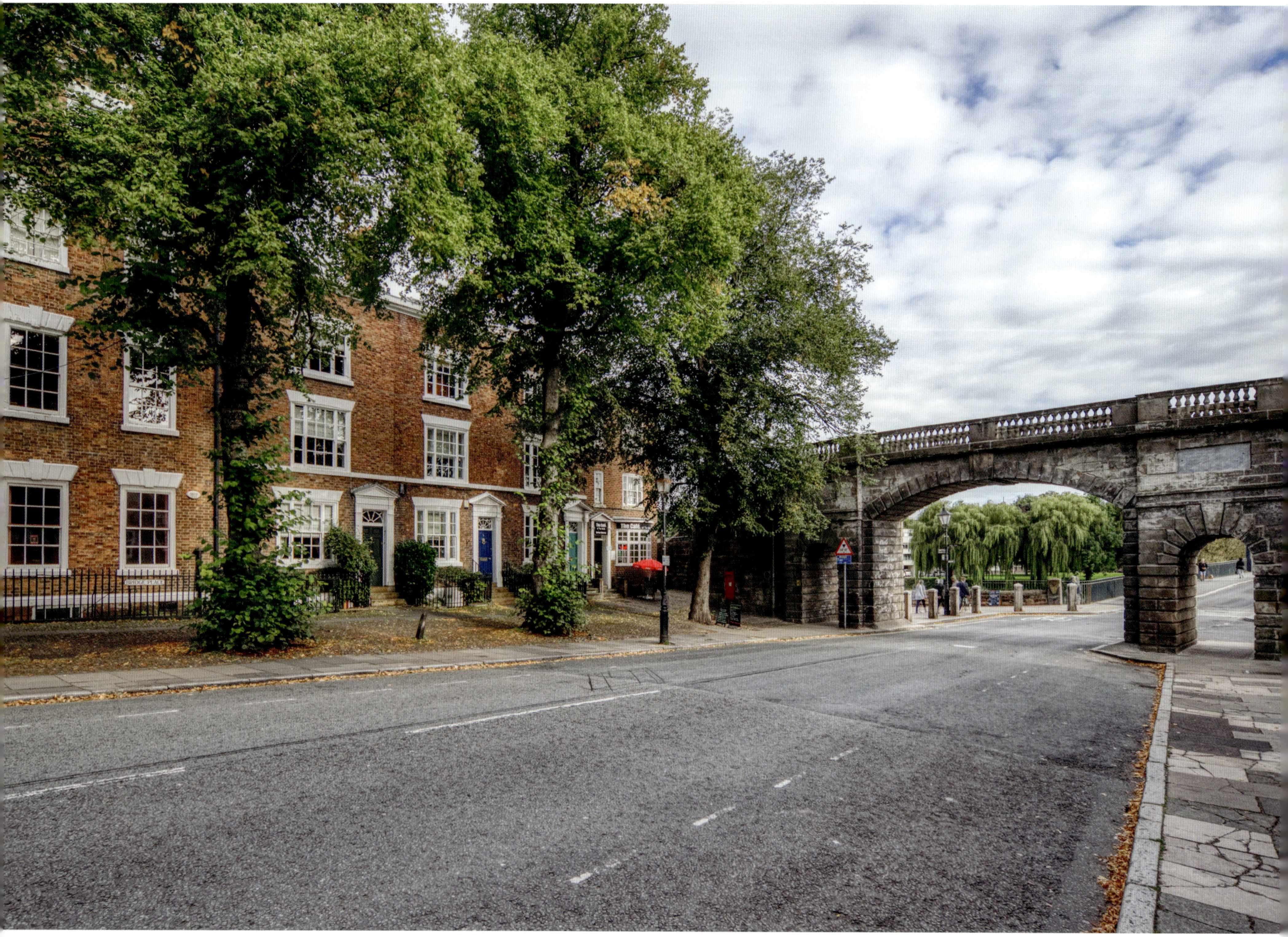

| BRIDGE PLACE |

A walled oasis
in the heart of the city...

Fall in love before you even set foot inside No. 9 Bridge Place. Set to the backdrop of Chester's ancient Roman walls and across from sixteenth century, black and white timbered, Bear and Billet pub, there is a profound sense you are entering 'Ye Olde Worlde Chester'.

No. 9, Bridge Place is a Grade II listed, landmark Georgian home set over five levels (including cellar). Beside the city walls and within striking distance of the river, this treasured home has a history inextricably woven into Chester's rich tapestry.

Built in the mid 1700s, Bridge Place embodies Georgian grace. Respectfully renovated using local firms, over an 18-month period floors have been reconnected to restore No. 9 into one grand five-story home. Beyond the seamlessly smooth edifice is a home where windows have been replaced and refurbished, walls replastered and flooring reinforced. The result? A home that bridges the centuries, where heritage features sit comfortably amongst contemporary, lifestyle enhancing accompaniments.

BRIDGE PLACE

A tale of two sides of the city to the ground floor; the bay window of an intimate lounge to the front frames views over the Tudor stylings of Chester. To the rear, beyond the archway, a modern kitchen-dining room directs the eye out through glass bifolds to the exotic landscaped garden of well-tended bushes and loquats; a walled oasis in the heart of the city.

A city sanctuary seemingly designed for pre-drinks and after parties, the locally fitted kitchen is reassuringly well-stocked with wine cooler, instant boiling taps and a central island facing the dining area for maximum sociability.

Skylights, vaulted ceiling and bifold doors create a bright airiness echoed in the mature and private Georgian walled garden. Steps flanked by lush planting, lead to stone patios and secret gardens, providing pockets of privacy and escape; the relaxing flow of the River Dee dampening the sounds of the city. A garden where it is never night, lighting creates a tropical midnight forest.

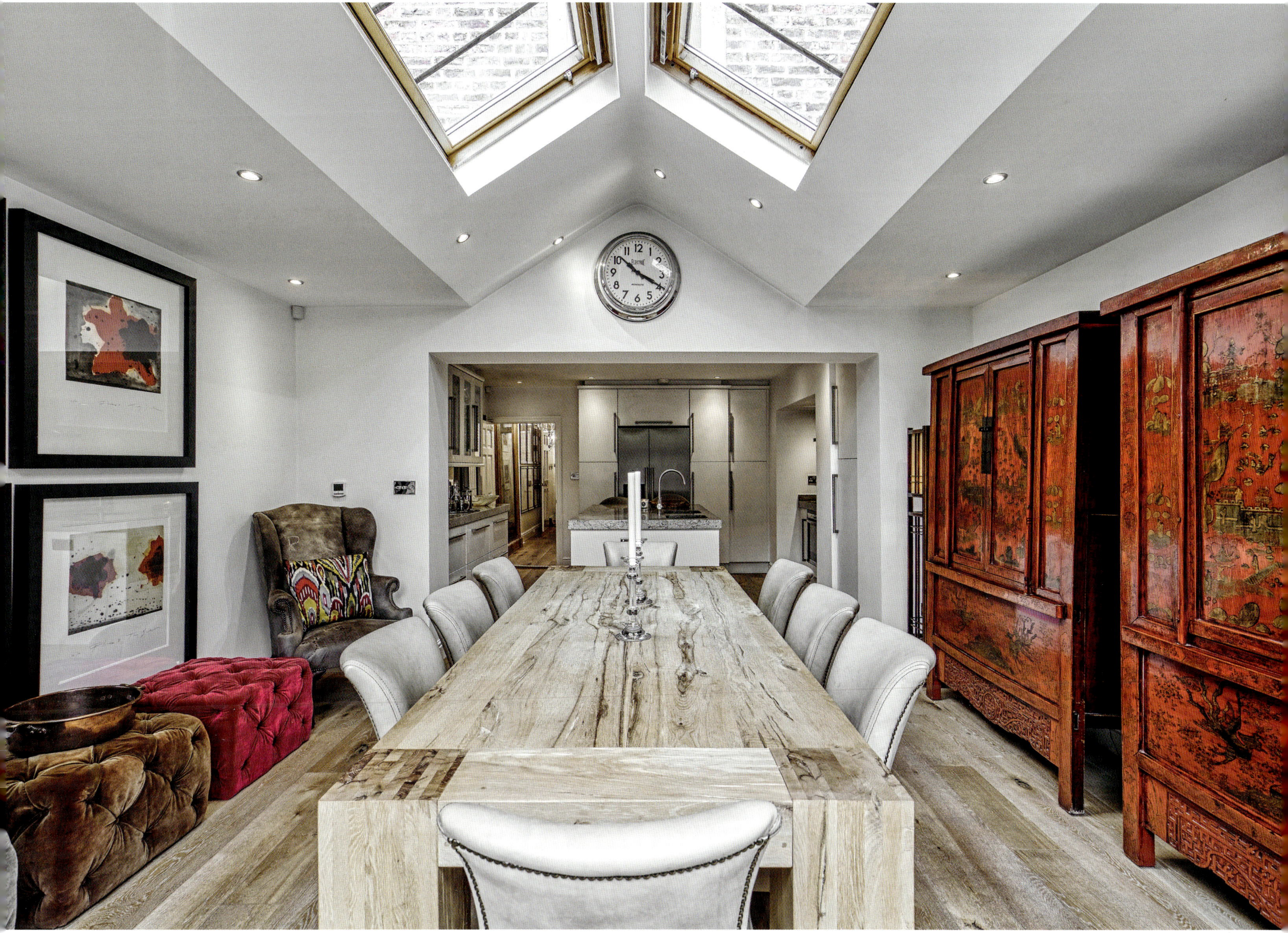

| 25 UNIQUE HOMES OF CHESTER |

| BRIDGE PLACE |

In the cellar, original cobbles combine with contemporary lighting and plumbing, while on the upper floors, chandeliers and beams dress blissful bathrooms and bedrooms with views out over the city walls and river.

True to its name, No. 9, Bridge Place links old and new, preserving and celebrating the historic nature of the home, whilst future proofing it for generations to come. (Cat5 wiring features throughout alongside excellent fibreoptic broadband service).

Setting and home work as one; the Roman walls within eyesight, the River Dee, Meadows and Chester Racecourse all but a stroll away - across the way, the black and white timbered edifice of the Bear and Billet, dating from the 1600s, itself steeped in history (it was the birthplace of John Lennon's grandmother). Past, present and future all align at Bridge Place.

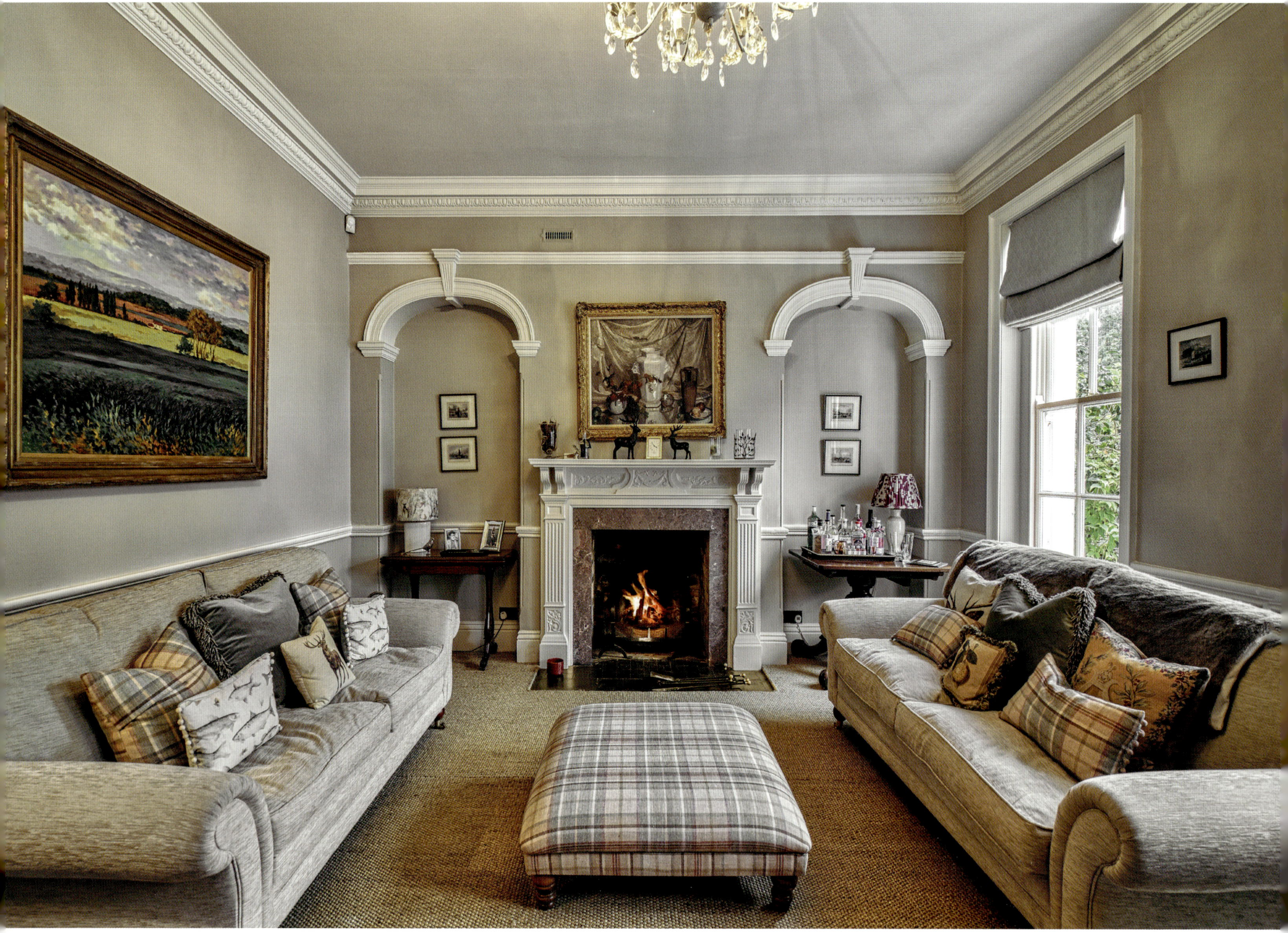

DEE BANK HOUSE

Gothic revival meets regency grandeur...

Wrapped up history, mystery and lusciously landscaped gardens, Dee Bank House is a home whose captivating position overlooking the River Dee has led to many musings regarding its origins. Rumoured to have once been connected to the local church by tunnel, its position beside Farndon Bridge - a significant border between England and Wales – gives the distinct impression Dee Bank House was purpose built for this 'look out' location in days gone by (lent kudos, in part, by the odd bullet hole in the stone walls).

Originally encompassing 60 acres and a proportion of riverbank, traits of its Georgian origins can be witnessed in the shuttered, Gothic revival bathroom windows and the Regency grandeur of the towering, curved columns, viewed at their most impressive from far down the garden. Retaining, restoring and reinstating heritage features is a diligent process that dates back as far as Dee Bank House's 1927 owners; the custodians past and present share one common trait: a duty of care and respect for the Grade II listing of this handsome home.

| DEE BANK HOUSE |

Handsome without and within, echoes of the Georgian heritage remain in the high ceilings, ornate plasterwork and auspicious rams' heads carvings, etched above solid mahogany doors. Vintage feel touches – cast iron radiators and limestone flooring – create an impactful impression upon arrival. Yet homely too. Dee Bank House shuns imposing, instead issuing a warm and homely welcome to those who cross its threshold. Character is retained in the heritage palette throughout (think Little Greene's Tea with Florence and the classical Georgian tones of Farrow & Ball's Inchyra Blue), whilst subdued lighting resists the urge to invite illumination into every corner.

Maintaining character, the sitting room retains an imposing feel, even the sunny and bright kitchen keeps one foot in tradition with its hearty Aga, its lustre amplified by spotlighting. Nothing is twee. Old and new in happy accord.

Rooms interconnect and flow; music, entertaining and formal dining rooms meet whilst doors allow the family room to be closed off from the kitchen, for cosy mornings reading the paper by the Georgian gothic fireplace. An inner hallway serves as a hub, its enormous painted crockery cabinet a clue to its heritage in the servants' quarters.

| 25 UNIQUE HOMES OF CHESTER |

| DEE BANK HOUSE |

| DEE BANK HOUSE |

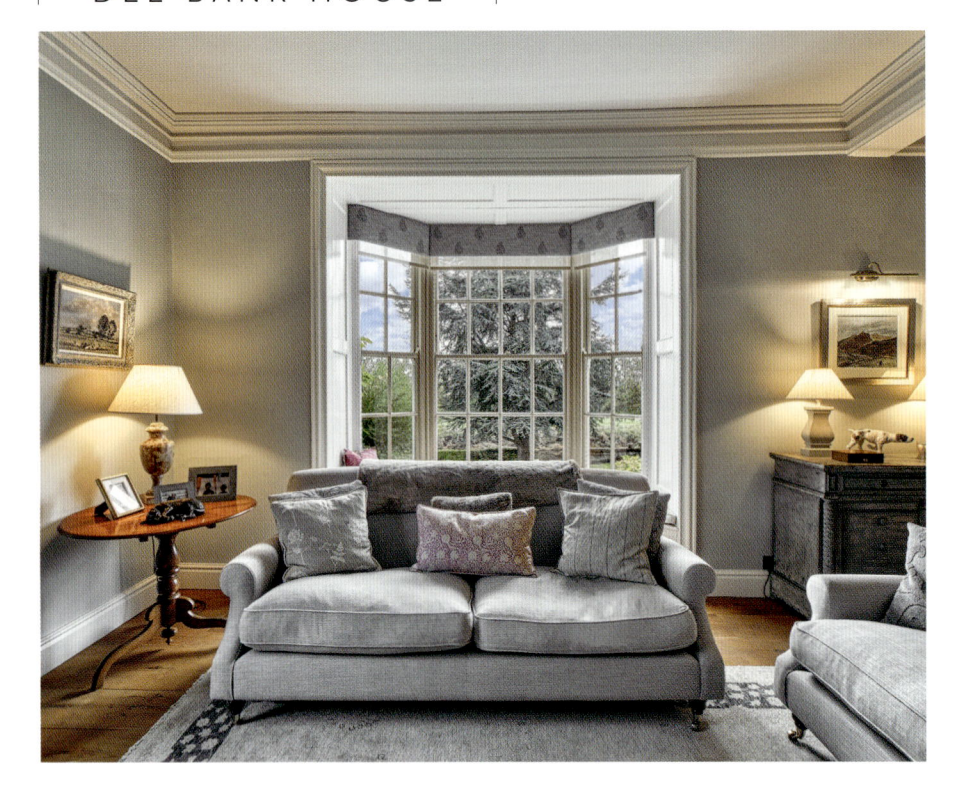

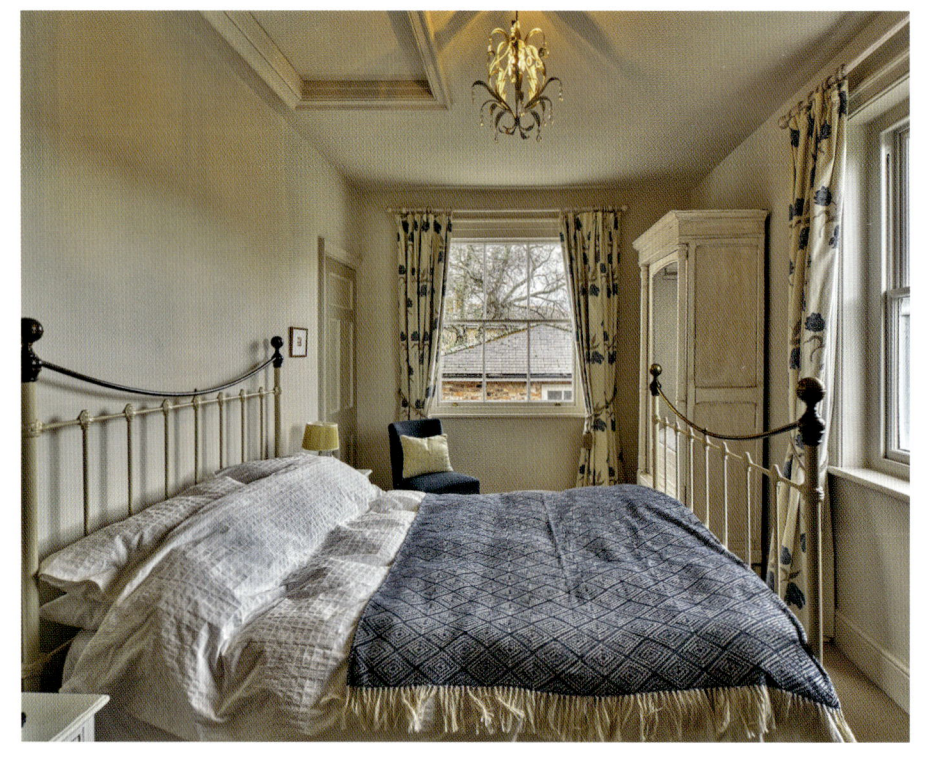

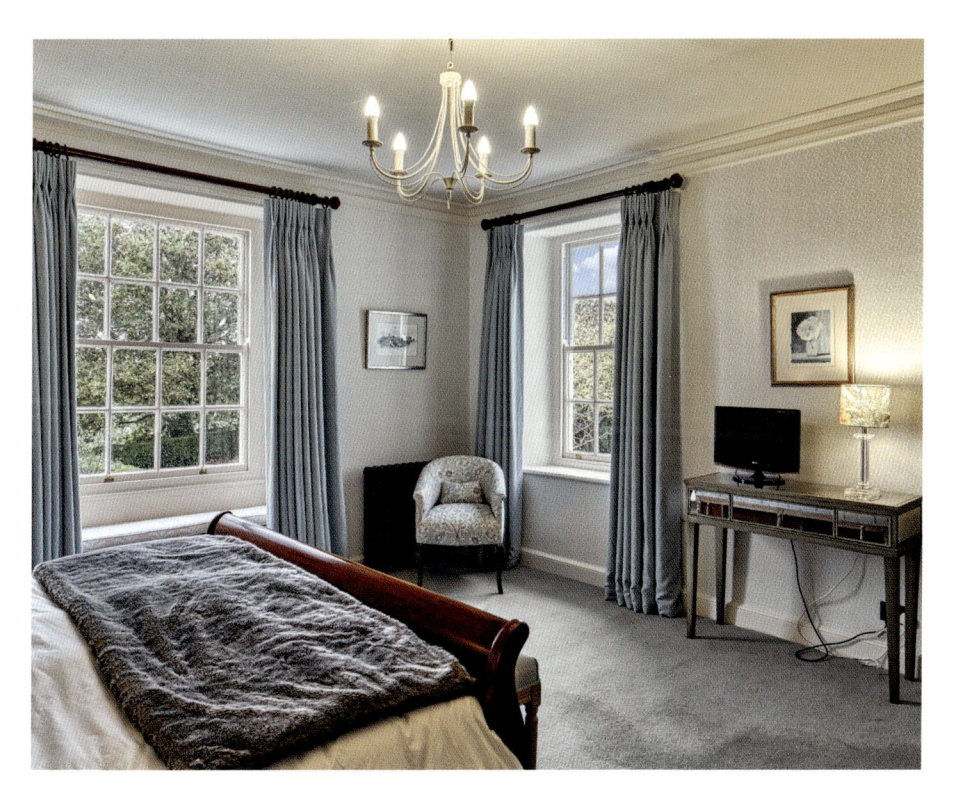

Outside, four acres of gardens reveal more history. Built into the sandstone of the cliff face – a Site of Special Scientific Interest – is an icehouse, with its arched oak door and stone carved fox head. Sandstone steps lead down to the riverbank, and a paved, pergola covered patio with a Mediterranean vibe. Deep wells in the garden are reminders of its proximity to the water, where a spring on the riverbank once quenched locals. A public footpath runs along the riverbank to Aldford, with Chester only a walk - or kayak – away.

Box hedging provides a pretty outlook from the sandstone window by the stairs, whilst winding wisteria and tropical-toned Cordylines counterpose. Beside the driveway, a dell carpeted in snow drops heralds spring, chased by fragrant wild garlic.

Beautiful throughout the seasons, Dee Bank House is a home which sparks to life in the presence of people. Passed down, cherished and protected through the generations, the duty of which is a privilege to perform.

| 25 UNIQUE HOMES OF CHESTER |

| 68 TARVIN ROAD |

Fearlessly bold
and challenging conceptions of conformity...

Above the bustle of Tarvin Road stands a home proud to be unique. For beyond its austere gabled front, No. 68 is a home that unabashedly challenges the concept of conformity.

Built in 1884, No. 68 is a home existing in the now. Resisting the urge to reawaken its Victorian sensibilities, the intrepid attitude of its current owners is to leave their own historical imprint on the home. With the allowance of a few subtle nods towards the past, it is a home not defined by its antiquity.

Patricia Urquiola tiles make an impactful statement of floral, digital and geometric design in the entrance hallway; each tile unique "like Space Invaders". A bold and fearless statement of intent from the off, resonating throughout the home.

Embracing the Marie Kondo school of thought that the embellishments made to the home are more than just an act, but a feeling, emotive décor features in every room. Each element sparking joy. The result is a luxe feel, with metallic

68 TARVIN ROAD

tones of gold and brass; boutique chic, the opulence of bars and intimacy of boudoirs. "A little luxury in your own home."

As stand out spaces go, the kitchen is a true statement piece. Inspired by a visit to the Chelsea Design Centre, this bold, bespoke kitchen was born from close collaboration between owner, architect and Chester furniture maker Brownlow, morphing from black metallic to celebrate the understated elegance of plywood.

Eschewing traditionalism, Italian glamour emanates from the enormous porcelain Porcelanosa worktop; a perfect balance for the homely warmth of the lacquered and stained tobacco tones of the plywood cabinetry. Contravening conformity once more, the traditional trio of pendants above the island is superseded by a sextet Swedish lamps in the Niclas Hoflin designed Long John pendant, casually suspended on brown leather belts. The result? An urban city bar, that happens to have an oven and hob in it.

Statement lighting is of utmost importance within the scheme of décor at Tarvin Road, where ambient wall and ceiling illumination cast by Flos is as artful as it is practical.

From the kitchen, the picture window paints a panorama of the garden, flat, long and lush, a serene space that provides peace at a glance, nature's constant.

Indoors, room flows on from room, taking inspiration from the vibrancy of flea markets, the splattergun surprise of charity shop hauls. Chic, and in no way shabby. Bold, brave and embracing its emotive design, No. 68, Tarvin Road is an eclectic home that dares to be seen.

| 25 UNIQUE HOMES OF CHESTER |

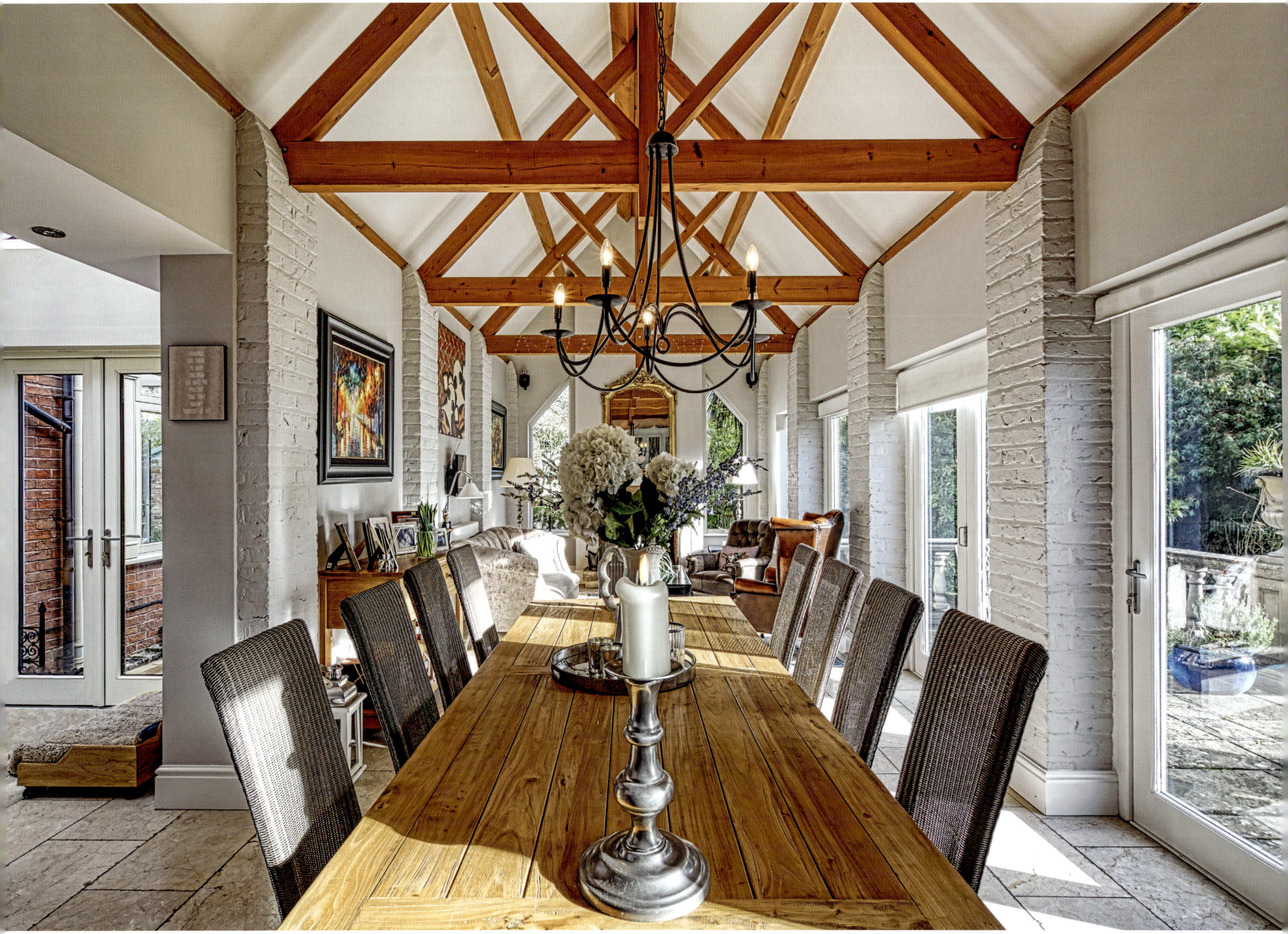

| WOODLAND HOUSE |

Striking the perfect balance...

Community is at the heart of Mollington, a picturesque Cheshire village on the cusp of Chester, the first place in Britain to adopt the Neighbourhood Watch Scheme.

Tucked tantalisingly back from the village lanes behind an enclave of green, Woodland House enjoys both the privacy of the village and the proximity to Chester, only a summer's day walk away through countryside.

Built for an esteemed local antique dealer in the mid-twentieth century, Woodland House strikes the perfect balance of convenience and rurality.

Much like the gardens within which it is set, Woodland House reveals itself slowly, room by room, inviting you deeper into the living areas found beyond the entrance hall. Almost Victorian in its depth, room leads on to room in delightful fashion.

WOODLAND HOUSE

Contemporary décor holds back slightly, retaining a traditional feel and evolving from room to room. In the entertaining lounge, the drama of Farrow & Ball's Stiffkey Blue provides an engaging backdrop to the deliciously droll artwork of Sarah Jane Szikora.

Winters are best enjoyed in the front lounge, where plaster coving and a roaring log burner provide a restful haven for retiring with a book, away from the bluster of the elements. Built-in bookshelves ensure ample choice of novel.

Reconfigured from its rabbit warren origins, becoming a home with easy flow, it is the kitchen and orangery, perhaps, that prompt the greatest gasps. Light dominates, flowing in through a series of French doors and roof lanterns, infusing the outdoors with the inside.

With all the welcome of a medieval banqueting hall, a curved breakfast bar mirrors the warmth in the exposed timber beams above the dining table, as the open fire crackles merrily within the hearth at the pinnacle of the scene.

A home that lends itself to entertaining, feast in the orangery, flowing outdoors onto the terrace in the summertime, or retire to the cinema room for a game of pool; everything flows at Woodland House, including the good times. A true family home, an annex has been created above the garage to deliver multigenerational living.

Woodland House lives up to its name, the many garden rooms echoing with birdsong while protected great crested newts make their home in the wildlife pond.

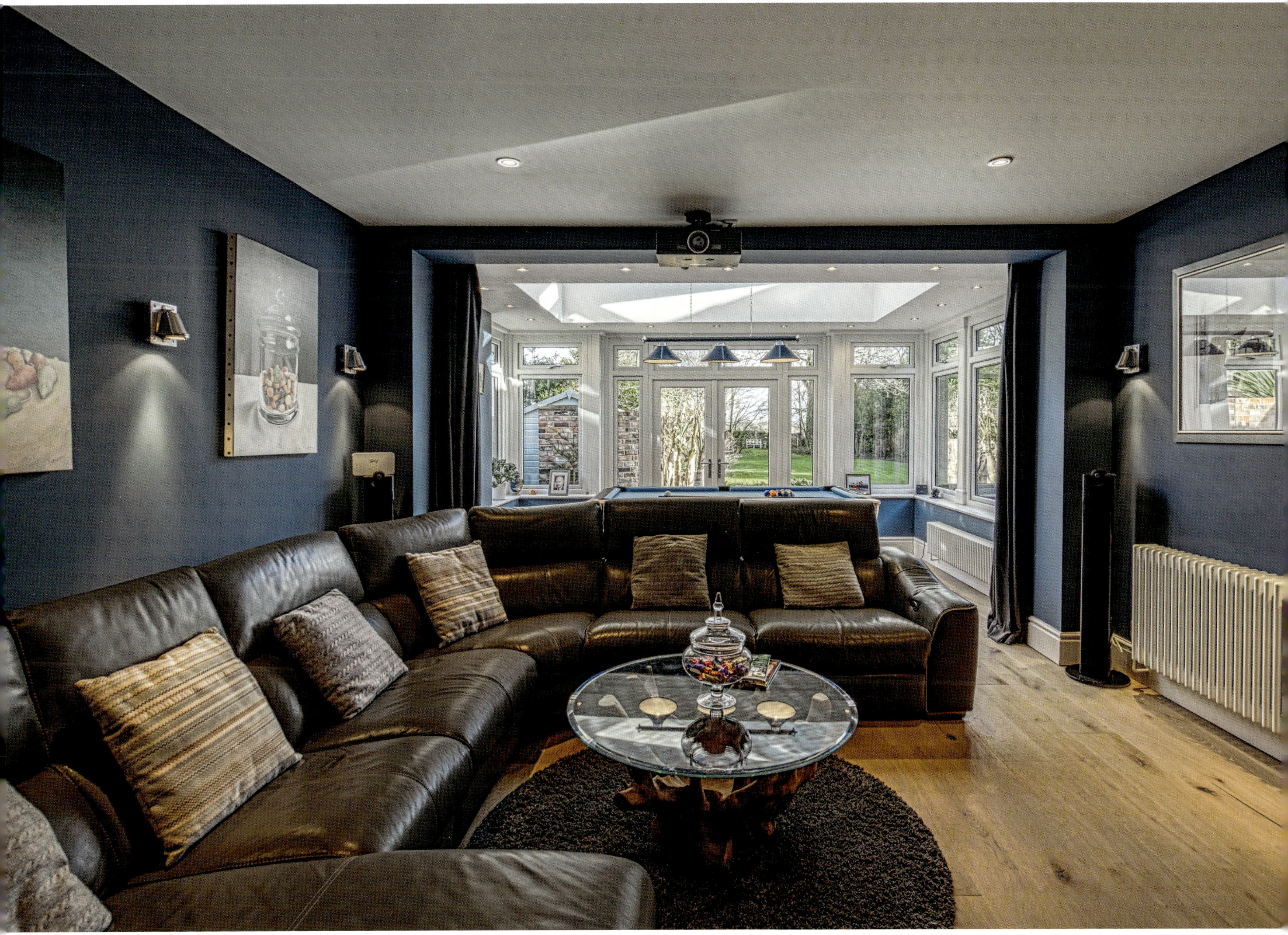

| 25 UNIQUE HOMES OF CHESTER |

WOODLAND HOUSE

Buffered to the rear by a bank of privately owned land, the privacy and security of Woodland House is absolute. A perfect balance of lawn for ball games, seating areas for rest and relaxation, and formal knot garden, the outdoors at Woodland House is as enchanting as the rooms within.

Woodland House in any other location would smell as sweet, yet within the peaceful, community-led village of Mollington, it takes on an even dearer perfection.

A family home at heart, providing pleasure and drawing companionship through its entertaining spaces, Woodland House is a more than a house, it is an experience to be shared.

| 25 UNIQUE HOMES OF CHESTER |

| SWEET CHESTNUT HOUSE |

A haven of calm,
where nothing else matters but family, home and a dog...

Along the miscellany of modern homes, new builds and period properties to grace Kelsall's Waste Lane, stands Sweet Chestnut House, modestly set back beyond a screen of pine trees.

Once an ugly 1930s duckling, the owners' vision to bestow symmetry and beauty upon Sweet Chestnut House, has been achieved with swan-like finesse.

Stripped to its basics, indoors and out, the design was to create a home more suited to its surroundings. Wrapped in two acres of garden, paddocks and woodland, Sweet Chestnut House is the focal point of the plot.

Extensions, new floors and several rearranged walls later, Sweet Chestnut House has been reborn a sociable family home and entertaining haven.

Behind a gabled portico, modern, with a hint of country casual, a calming neutral palette pervades within, invigorated by a splash of Stiffkey Blue in the master bedroom. A home directed by light; a collaboration of Little Greene, Farrow & Ball, Neptune and Zoffany paint coats the walls from room to room, working in harmony with the natural illumination.

SWEET CHESTNUT HOUSE

A wow factor entrance hall enhanced by panelling and candle-lit lanterns, creates a warm welcome. Embracing spaces greet you at every turn, from the plush blue sofa in the spacious sitting room with its bountiful, bay window views over Kelsall, down the plain and out to the hills of North Wales.

Exemplifying the need to move with the times, the relocated kitchen now sits conveniently on the right of the hall. Fluted, handblown Jim Lawrence lighting hangs above the smooth granite island on antique pewter chains, a timeless touch. Open and free flowing, dining, cooking and reclining combine in this contemporary space.

Mud bead chandeliers festoon the ceiling of the orangery, a cosy and bright space with its log-burning stove, beyond which two sets of French doors connect to the lush garden.

| 25 UNIQUE HOMES OF CHESTER |

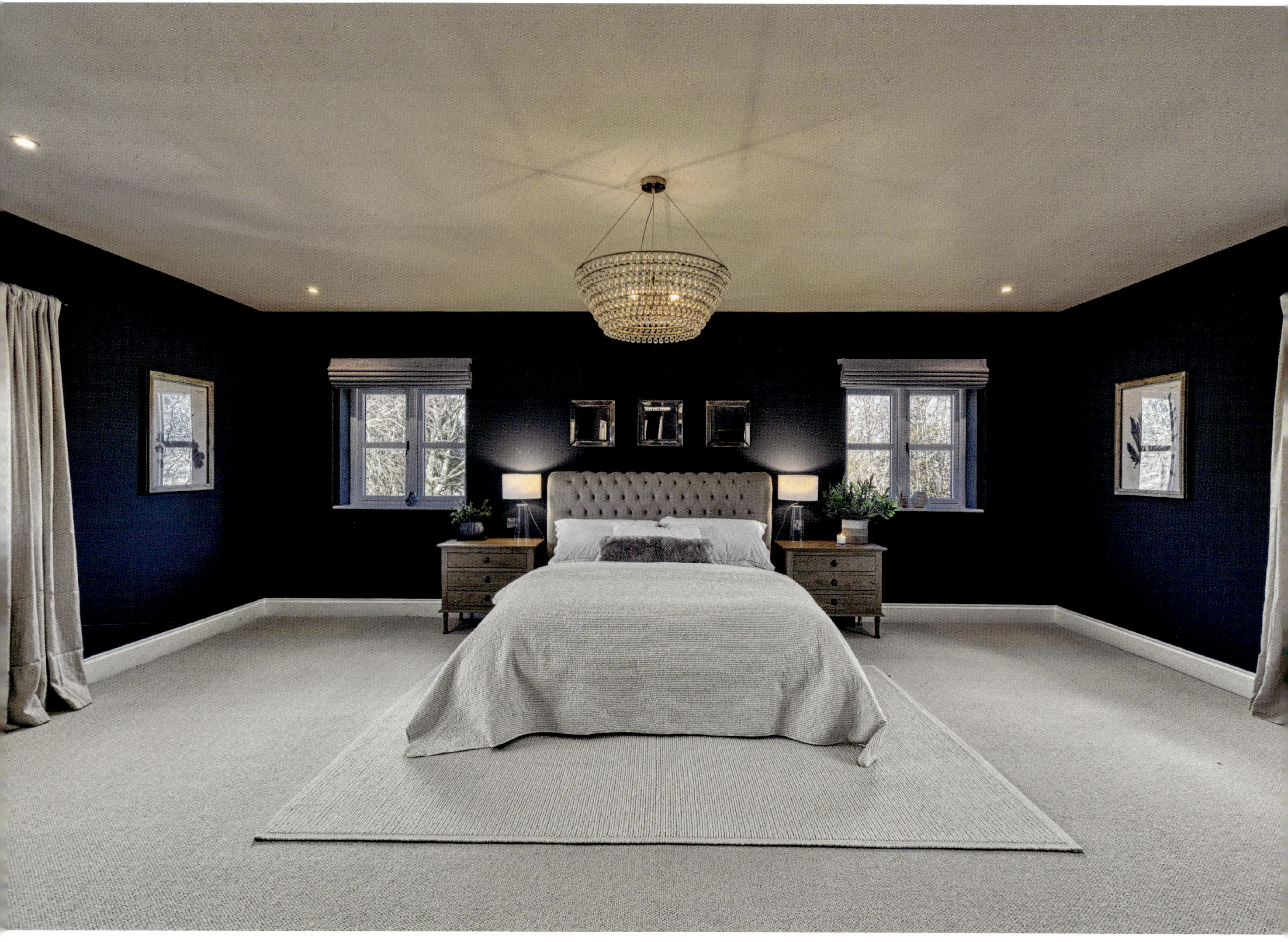

SWEET CHESTNUT HOUSE

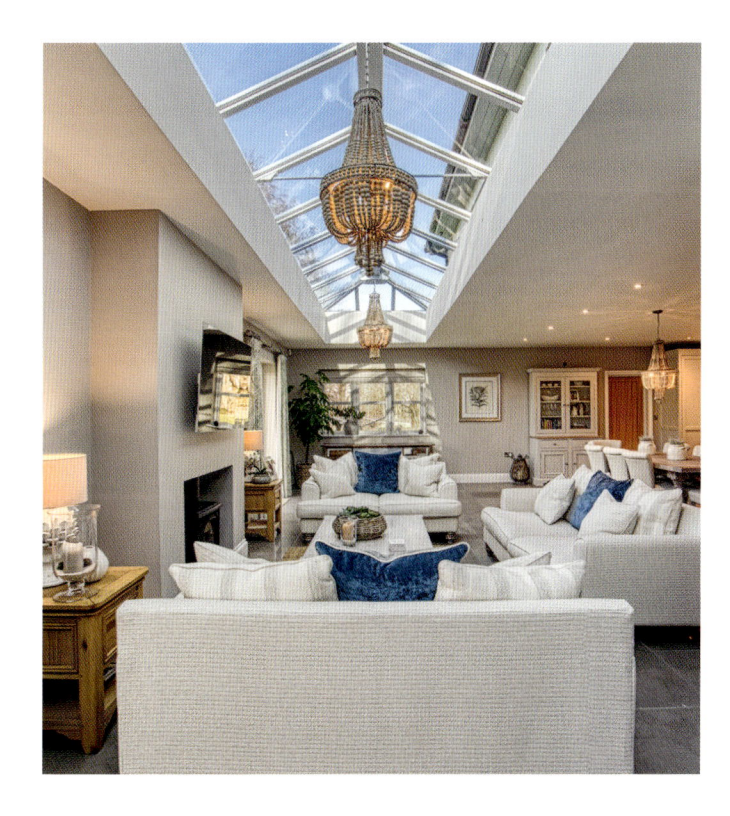

Sowing the seeds of love, the garden has also borne witness to the same devoted transformation as the home. A once dilapidated outdoor swimming pool has been reimagined as a sheltered, walled children's play area. Every inch of garden returfed and planted with olive trees and pretty shrubs, one tree takes pride of place, from which the home takes its name: Sweet Chestnut.

A rural retreat only 39 steps down into the village, Primrose Wood offers walks on the doorstep, for a home that works on every level.

At its heart, this reloved home has been repurposed as a haven of calm, where sunset views of mist covered hills evoke a sense of tranquility. A party home, an embracing space with an easy flow and feel, Sweet Chestnut House epitomises the things that matter most in life: family and home.

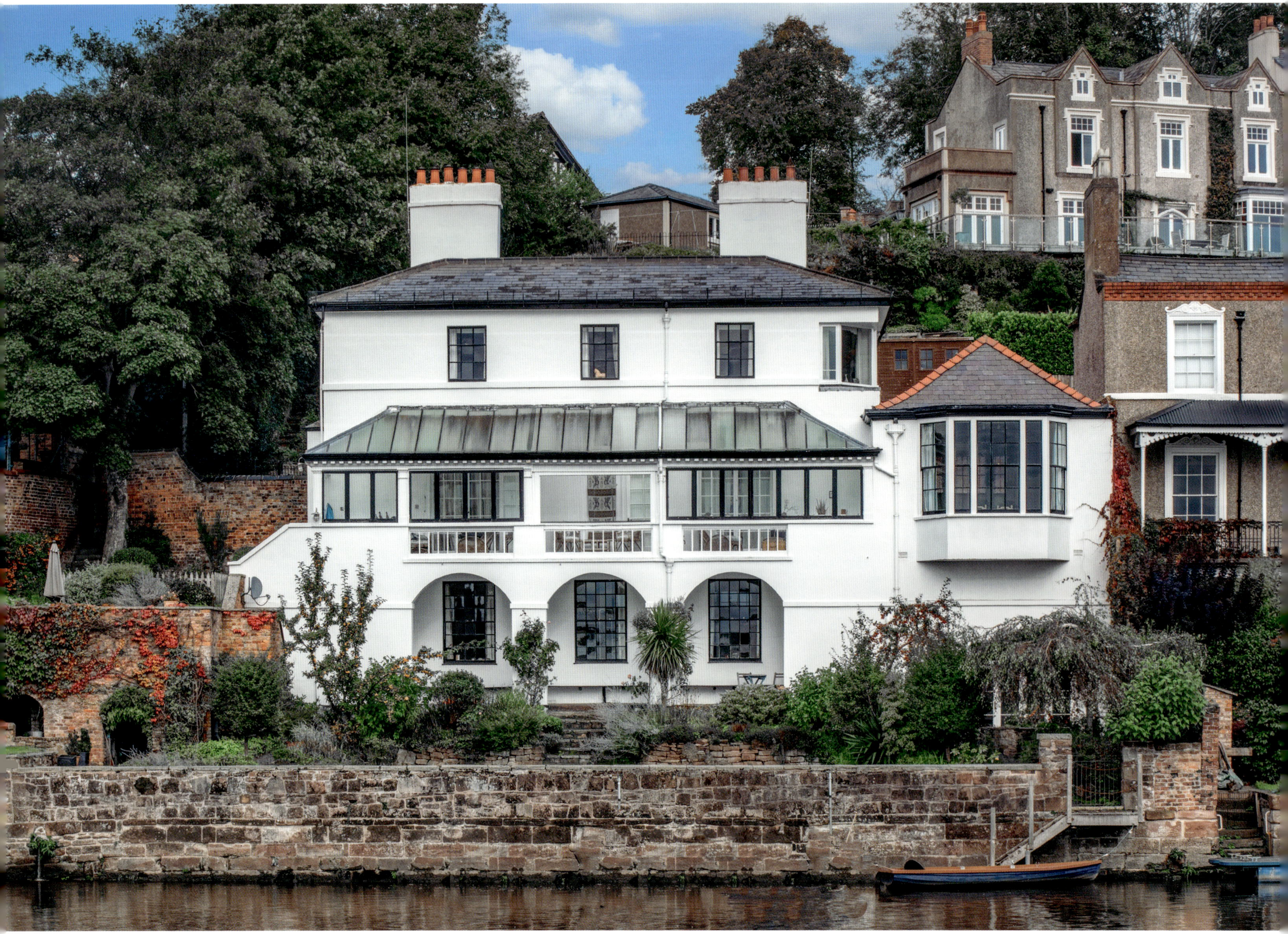

| CHESTER HOUSE |

Making a House a home...

An iconic piece of architecture showcasing its appealing Georgian symmetry, on the banks of the River Dee, Chester House is a standout home etched in local history.

Perhaps best viewed from The Meadows over the river, this well-photographed home dates back centuries, originally part of the Westminster Estate and sold to the Church Commissioners in 1866 to become the parsonage for the nearby and recently remodelled St Paul's Church. Prior to its sale, the land on which Chester House stands was part of the Barrel Well Hill brewery in Boughton, and whilst no evidence can confirm that Chester House is indeed the original abode, this Grade-II listed home's heritage features evoke an enchanting link to this era.

Renovated by its current owners who took up residence in the early 2000s, Chester House has been brought in line with a more modern style of living. Chester House is a home 'of its time', brimming with original features without feeling overtly ornate; a balance which embraces the most important quality of Chester House – its homeliness.

| CHESTER HOUSE |

Step inside and the craftsmanship of the nautilus curve of the carved staircase, sweeping up to the barrel-vaulted ceiling ahead is reminiscent of dinner parties where musicians fill the hall with fiddle music. Chester House is a spectacular home without pretentions of grandeur.

Banked into the hill, this middle level accommodates the main entertaining areas, including an open-plan homely kitchen-sitting room, the highlight of which is a bountiful bay window framing views out over the River Dee to The Meadows. Breaking the symmetry of the design, this space represents a 1900s complement to the residence, built on originally as a billiards room.

Decorative tones retain the vintage of Chester House, a cheerful uncomplicated palette alongside traditional oak parquet flooring. A home in harmony with its surroundings, large windows, notably in the formal drawing room and the 30 paned Georgian windows beneath the arches on the lower level (fitted with a wine cellar, gym and cinema room) retain a constant connection with the inimitable riverside views, inviting light and warmth in.

Views of the river dominate this predominantly south-facing home, to be savoured whatever the weather, from the verandah running the width of Chester House.

Upstairs a quirky corner window in the master bedroom perhaps offers the most impressive view, framing clear views along to the river's bend.

Gardens serve as an extension of the home, flowerbeds against the home step down to a level expanse of lawn beside the river wall, a handy buffer to prevent croquet balls succumbing to the river's flow. A verandah on one

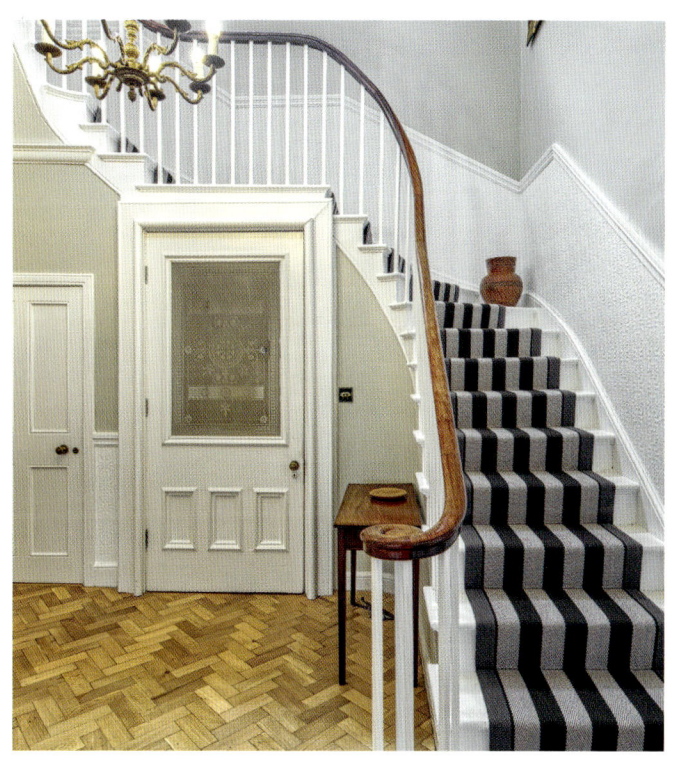

| 25 UNIQUE HOMES OF CHESTER |

| 25 UNIQUE HOMES OF CHESTER |

CHESTER HOUSE

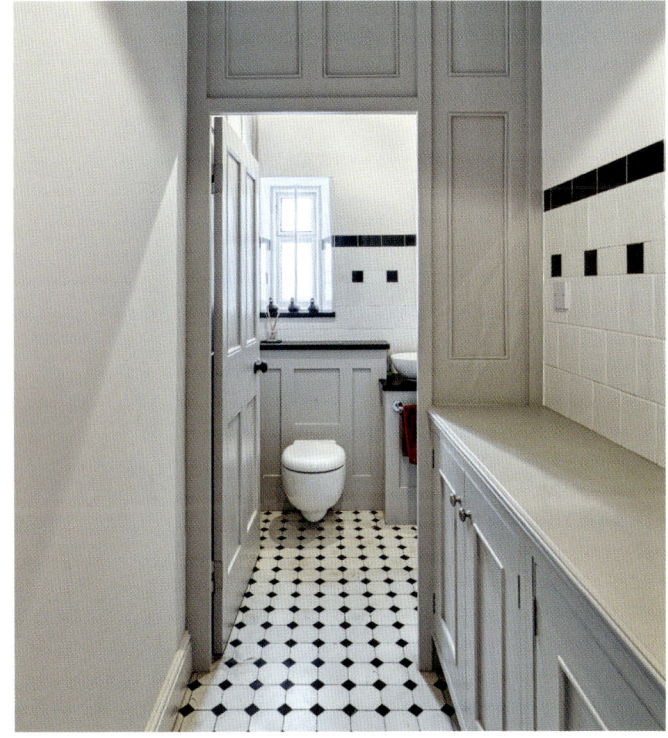

level offers a space to sit and relax and admire the views, whilst privacy from pleasure boats is provided by the entertaining area, with a firepit, tucked away out of sight of passers-by.

Three barrel vaulted tunnels in the garden connect to the home, conjuring tales of smugglers and stealthy riverboat trips taken under cover of night. Presumably storage for the former brewery, the tunnels add to the mystique of the home. Moorings at the foot of the garden are handy for trips to The Meadows and beyond. A passageway provides access to the garden when returning from walks, the old ferry path once used by those taking the rowing boat across from Handbridge to St Paul's Church.

A rural refuge; protected by the hill, the busy town centre is so close, yet seems a million miles away from tranquil Chester House.

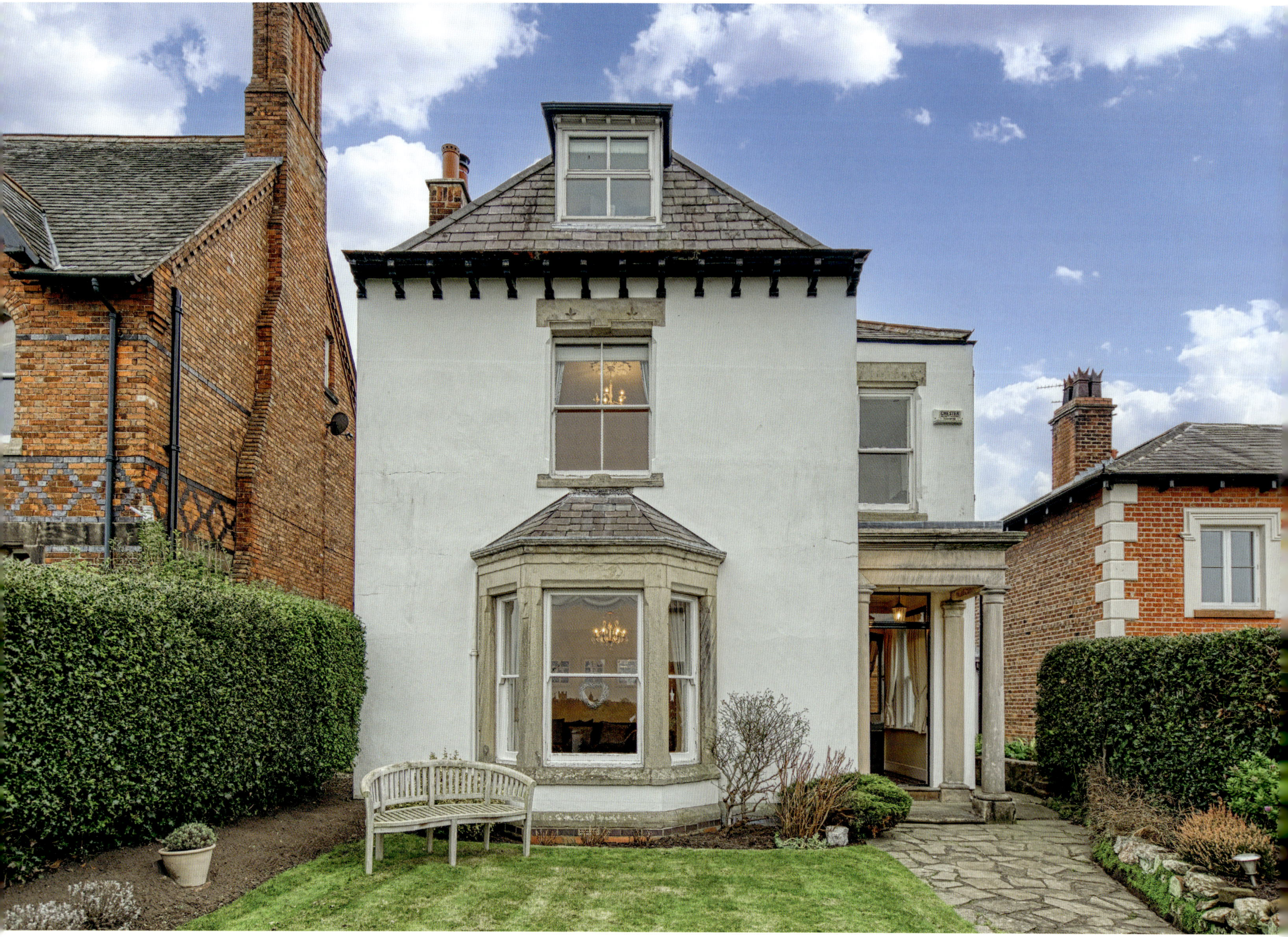

| 35 DEE BANKS |

The last house in Chester...

In summer, as the sun sets over the cathedral, the rooms of No. 35, Dee Banks are cast in bronze as the home burns orange in the fading light.

Overlooking The Meadows from high up above the banks of the River Dee, this late Victorian towering home enjoys the distinction of being the last house in Chester; a boundary stone outside the property marking the limits of the old city.

Built in 1875 on land once owned by the Chester Cathedral Canons as part of the Dee View Estate, the sun-kissed glow takes on an almost spiritual feel, when teamed with the medieval stained-glass iconography of the entrance hall.

Its elevated position plays a key role in its privacy, tucked behind a high hedge that does nothing to diminish the

35 DEE BANKS

river views, whilst providing a cloak of invisibility to the home. The path too is cleverly curved, offsetting the front door from the gate.

With the view behind you, the entrance hall comes as a surprise – broad and bright, belying expectations of the traditional 'long and narrow' Victorian hallway. Traditionality comes in the high ceiling, the elegant cornicing and plaster roses and the expanse of Minton tiling underfoot. The kitchen also 19th century in design, currently awaits a planned extension into contemporary family-dining-kitchen, opening out to the lawned, walled garden, which soaks up sunshine throughout the morning.

A home in sync with its surroundings, follow the arc of the sun round to the front in the afternoon, where light streams in through the bay window of the living room. A home with flow, lounge, garden room, kitchen and study all offer enough space for a family to live in harmony, coming together and moving apart like the tide. Where some unadulterated Victorian homes, with their long and deep design, can at times feel disconnected, 35 Dee Banks feels broad and balanced; a quirky home, relieving Victorian grandeur of its rigidity and transforming it into a comfortable family nest.

Following the polished curve of the bannister up, calm descends as you ascend, the height of the ceilings upliftingly light. Waking up in the morning, looking down on the world not looking in on you, birds hover on thermals, a reminder of the eyrie height Dee Banks occupies over the water.

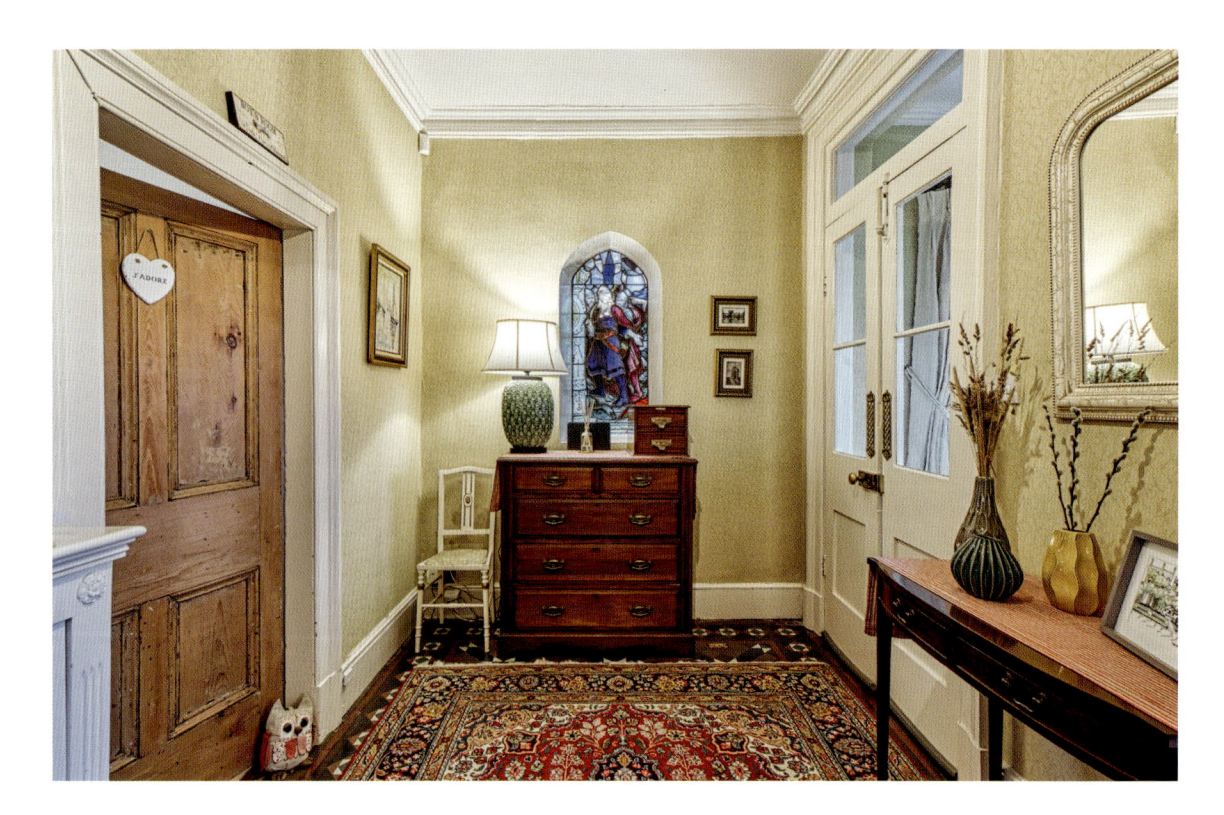

Bedrooms blossom into walk-in wardrobes and ensuite bathrooms. Upon the uppermost floor, office space and sleeping quarters combine in a myriad of rooms. To the rear, views of Bishops Field while to the front, the River Dee melts into The Meadows with vistas as far as the Clwydian Range and the distinguished crown of Moel Famau.

As evening falls, migrate from rear to front garden and over the road to the sloping lower garden, then beyond to the Sailing Club and the River Dee. 35 Dee Banks, the last house in Chester, where countryside and city meet and the rotation of the sun dictates the pace of life.

| 25 UNIQUE HOMES OF CHESTER |

Acknowledgements

This book owes its existence to a friendship dating back five years. I heard about Sam Ashdown through her inspiring Home Truths blogs. Sam is innovative, very fast paced and I am forever grateful that she cajoled me to follow my dream and so Currans Unique was born.

I want to say a heartfelt thank you to our wonderful team at Currans: Ashley, Ella, Cat, Lionel (Dad), Lucy, Meg, Sophie and Tim. Also a huge thank you to our awesome creative team: Adrian, Alex, Hope, Jaime, Mark and Sarah. I am so grateful and love working with you, and I am proud of what you do every day.

A particular mention is due to Sarah Igo and Adrian Little for their overall contribution. To Sarah for conducting the interviews and writing the inspiring words featured in these pages and to Adrian for capturing the homes so beautifully and perfectly, including your care and meticulous attention during hours of editing. Thank you to Maggie for the hours of careful editing and proofreading. Enormous thanks to the generous owners who have allowed us into their homes over the years, especially those who are quoted or pictured in the book.

Thank you to the brilliant Michael Byrne and Marius Herbert for their creativity and support. I am also grateful to Karen Hughes, from Printer Trento, for her expert guidance and encouragement especially at the gestation of the project and for keeping it on track. I must end with a huge thank you to my rock, my husband, John. This journey with you is thrilling. Thanks for saying yes.

Written by: Sarah Igo

Photography: Adrian Little

Design & Print Production: Michael Byrne & Marius Herbert

First edition: May 2022

Printed in Italy by Printer Trento

Produced by Zest Publications

ISBN: 978-0-9933206-8-2

Copyright © Currans Unique Homes 2022

All rights reserved. No part of this book may be reproduced or transmitted in any form, or by any means, electronic or mechanical, including photocopying, or stored in a retrieval system without the prior permission of the copyright holder. For permission requests write to the copyright holders at: sales@curranshomes.co.uk

CURRANS
unique homes

www.curransunique.co.uk

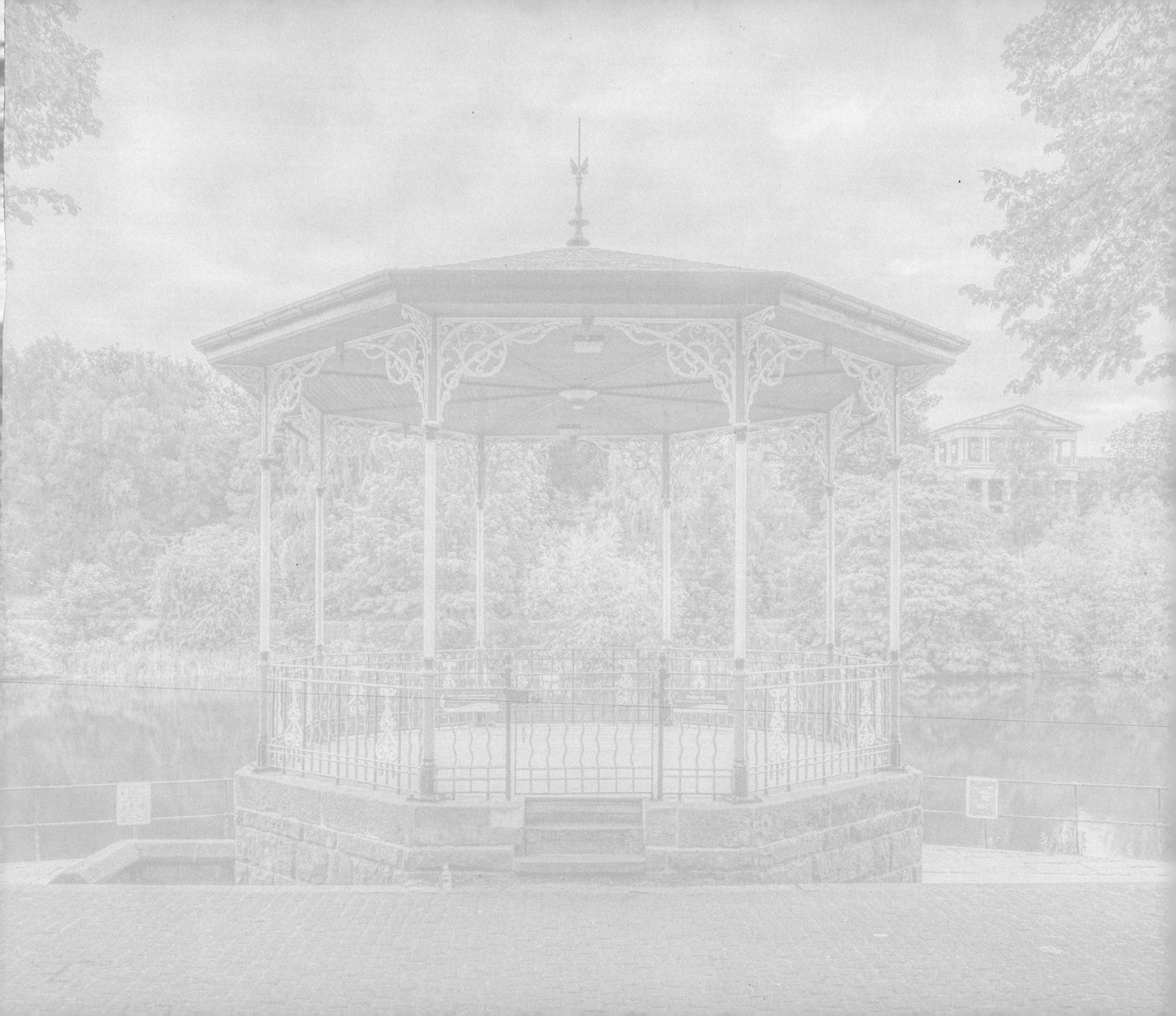

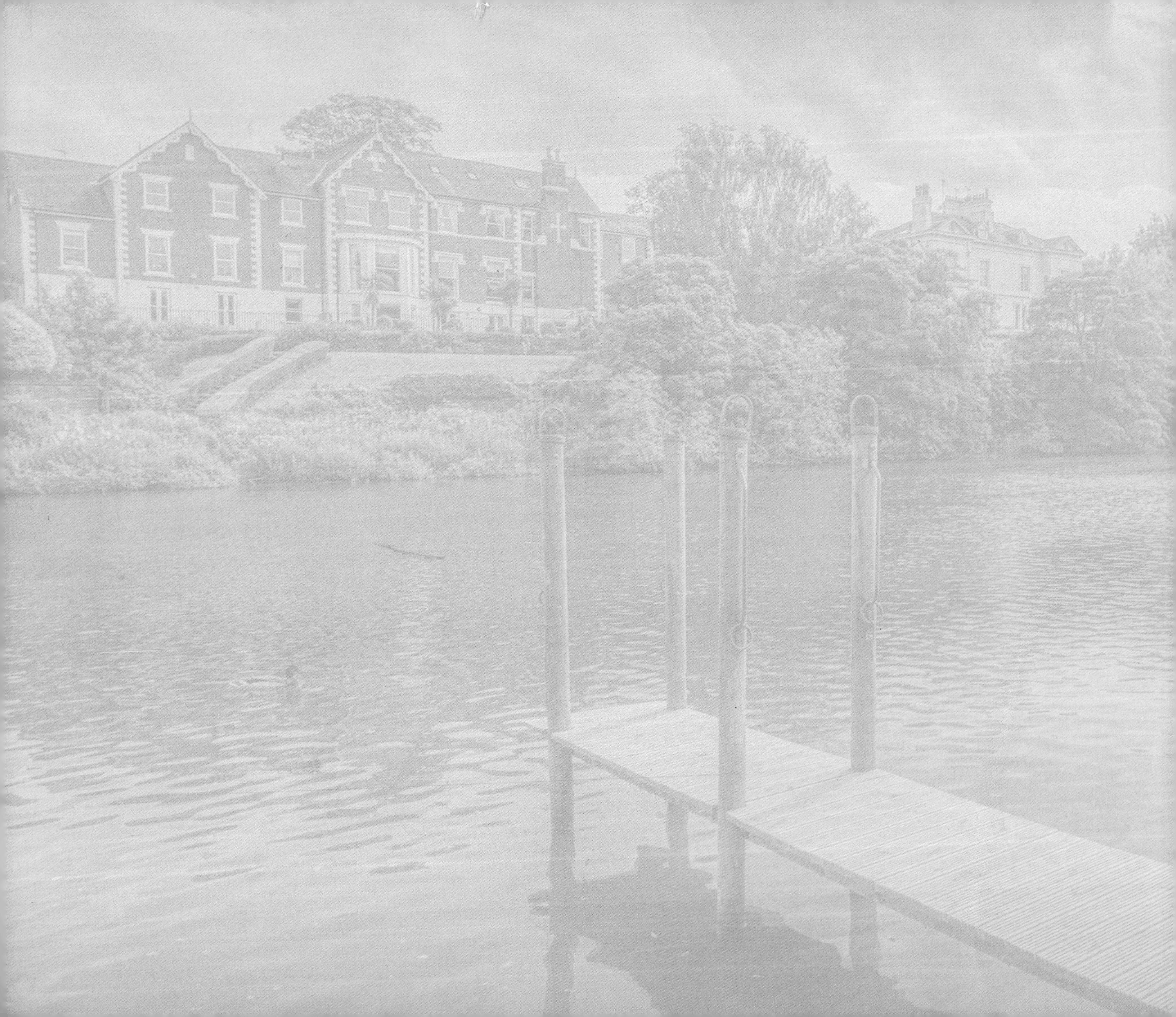